KAWAII
COLORING BOOK
Japanese style doodle coloring pages for relaxation

COPYRIGHT SMILING RAINBOW PRESS

SAMPLE PREVIEW PAGES

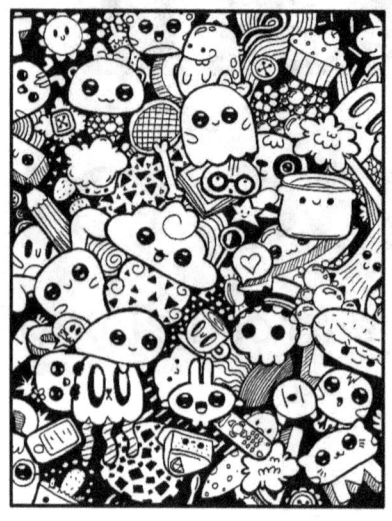 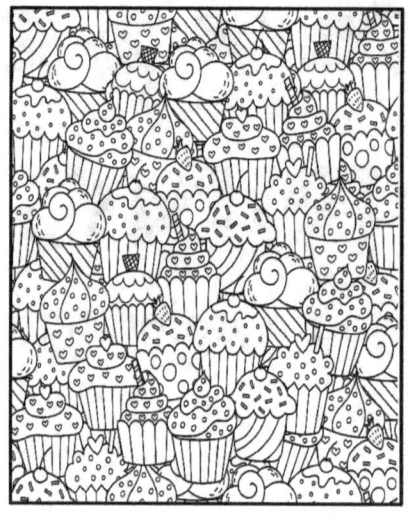 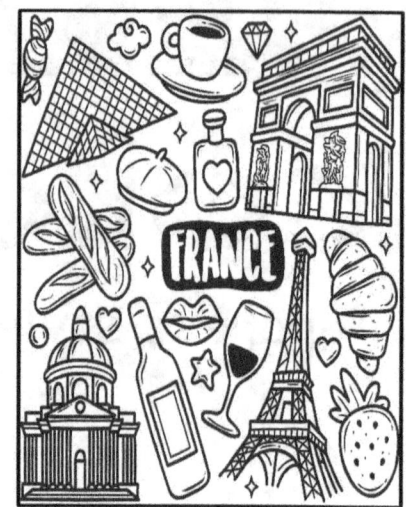
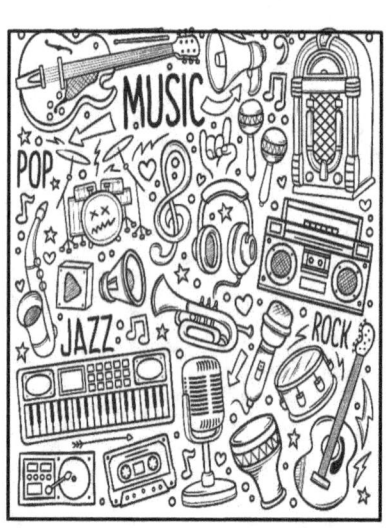 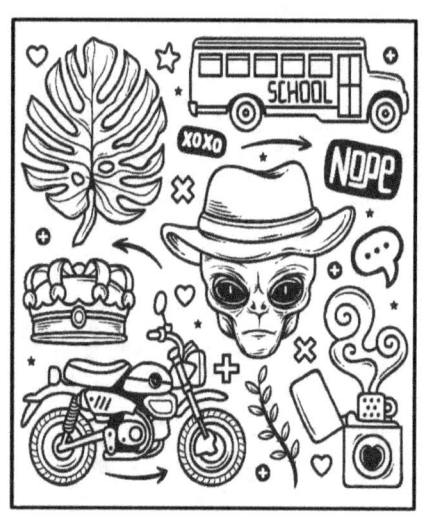 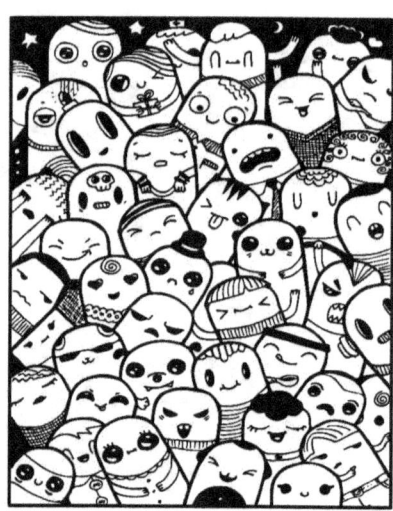
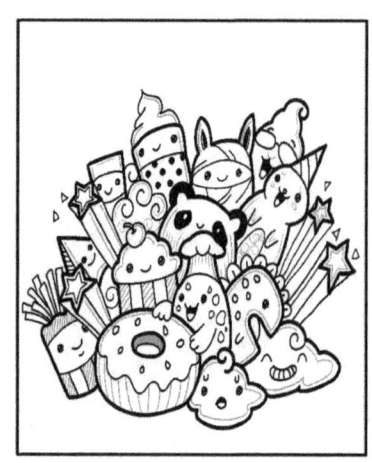 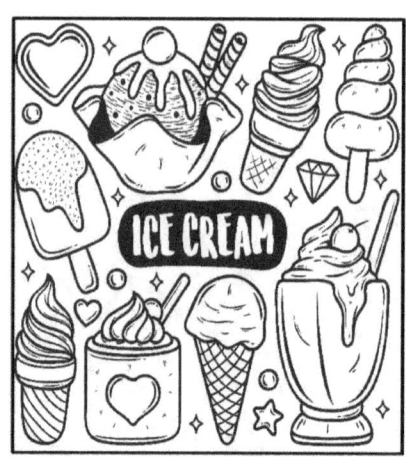

COLOR TEST PAGE

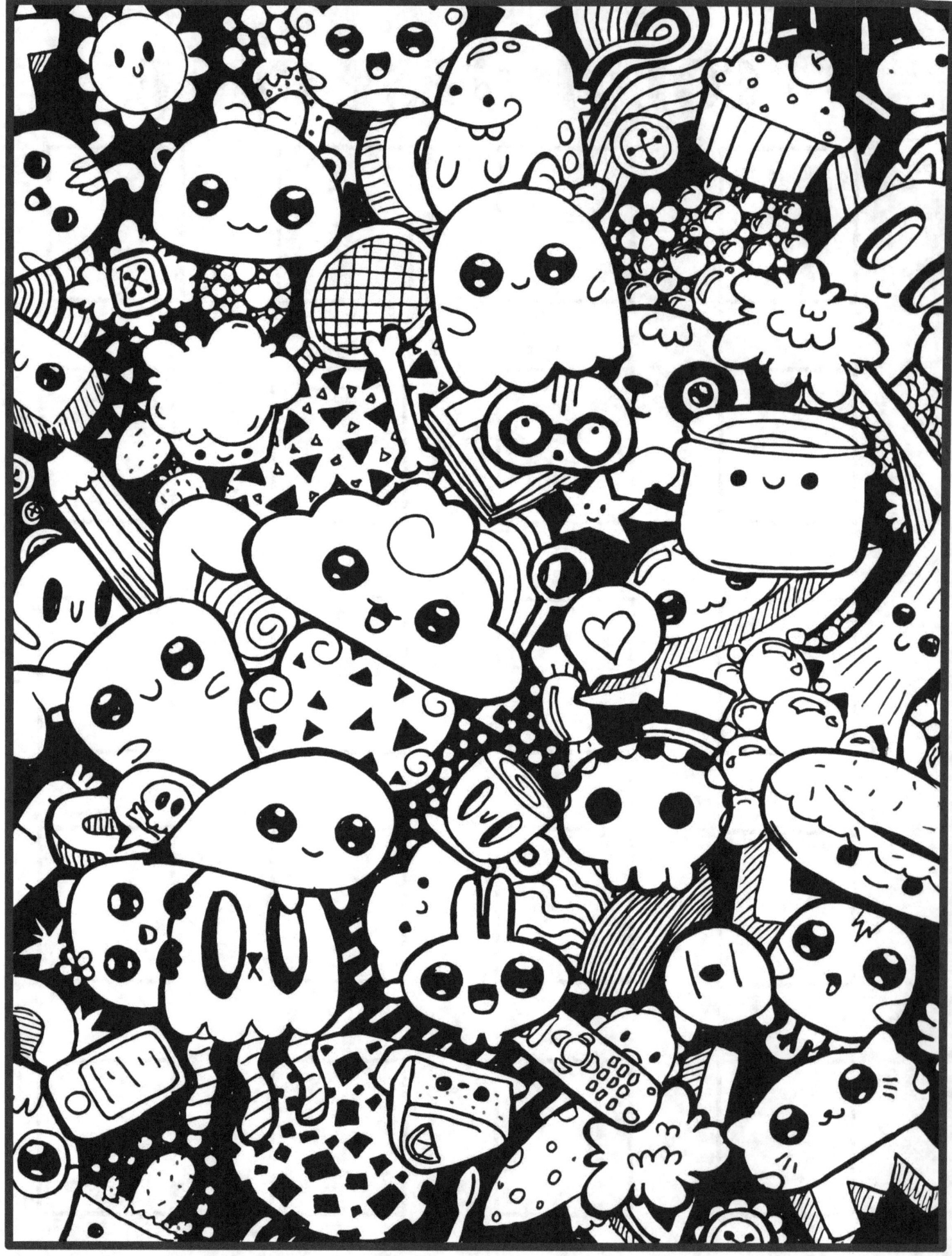

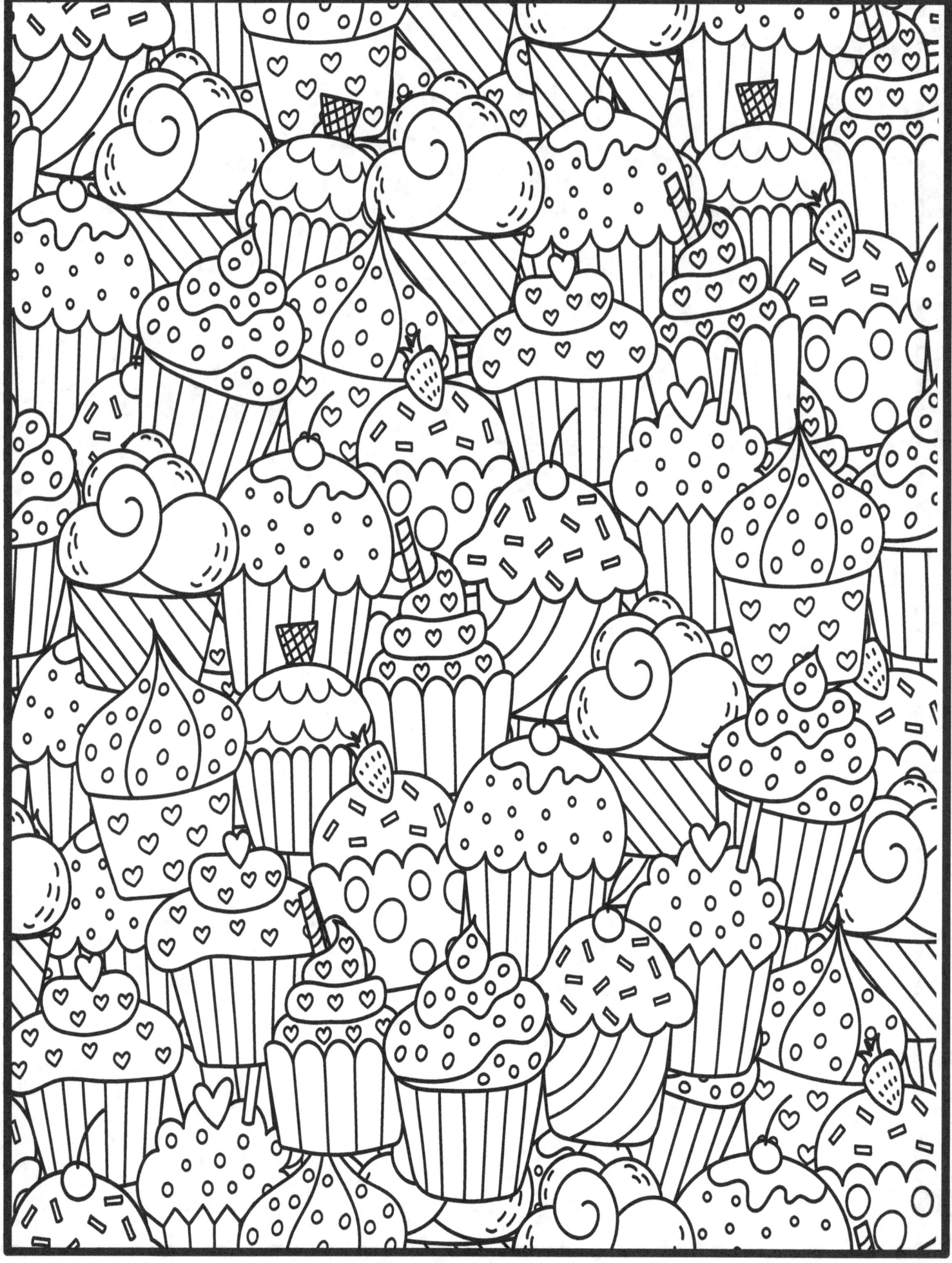

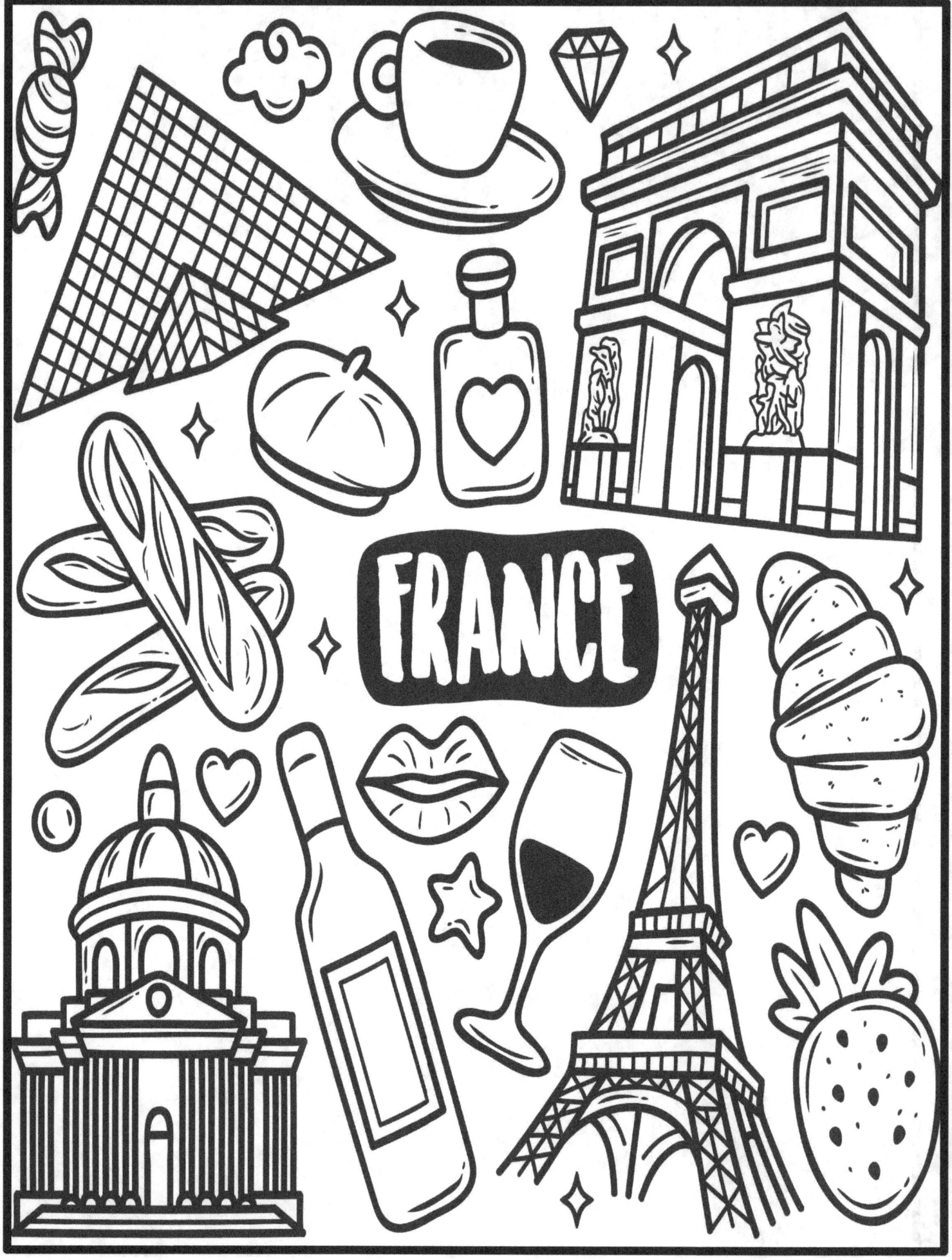

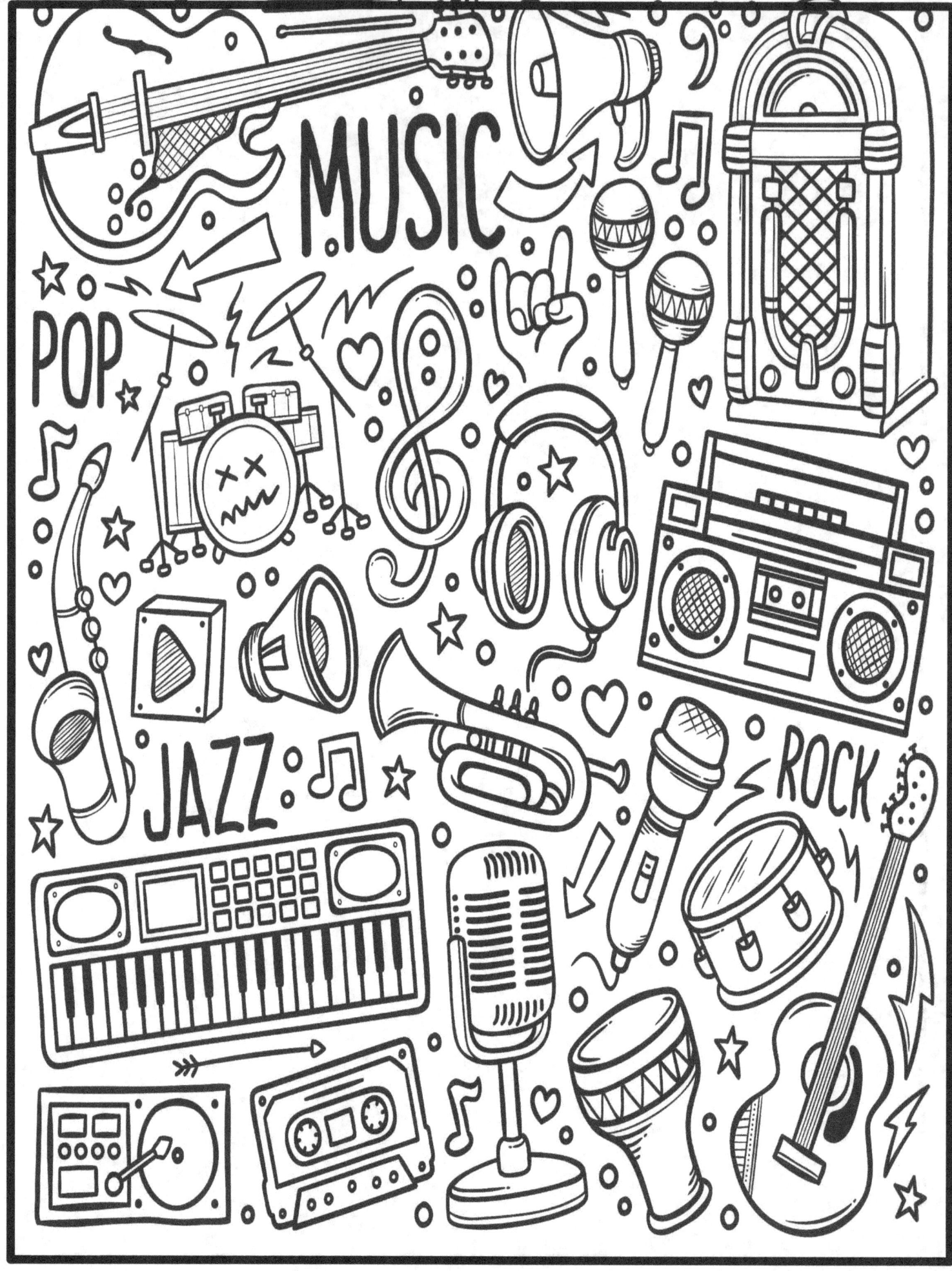

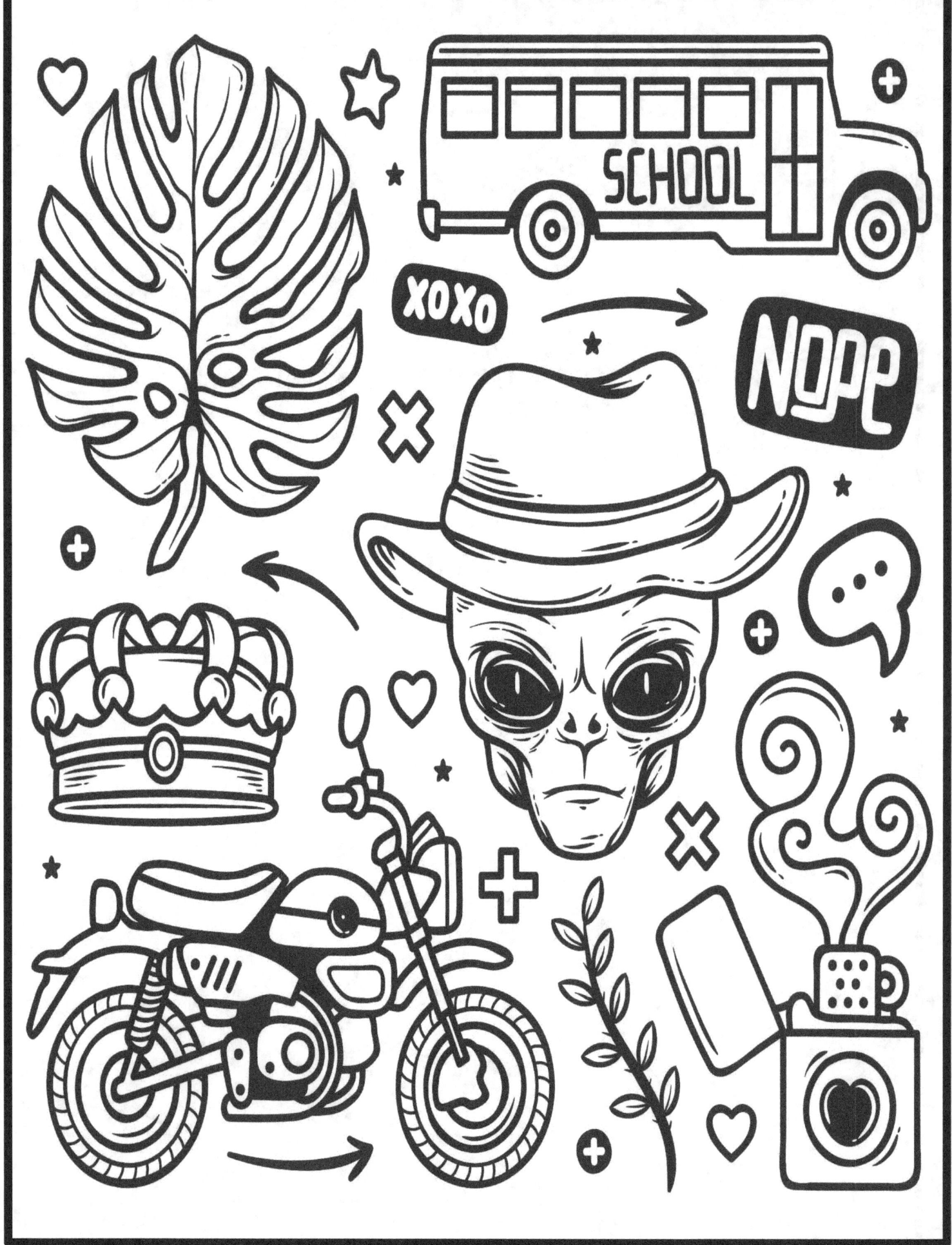

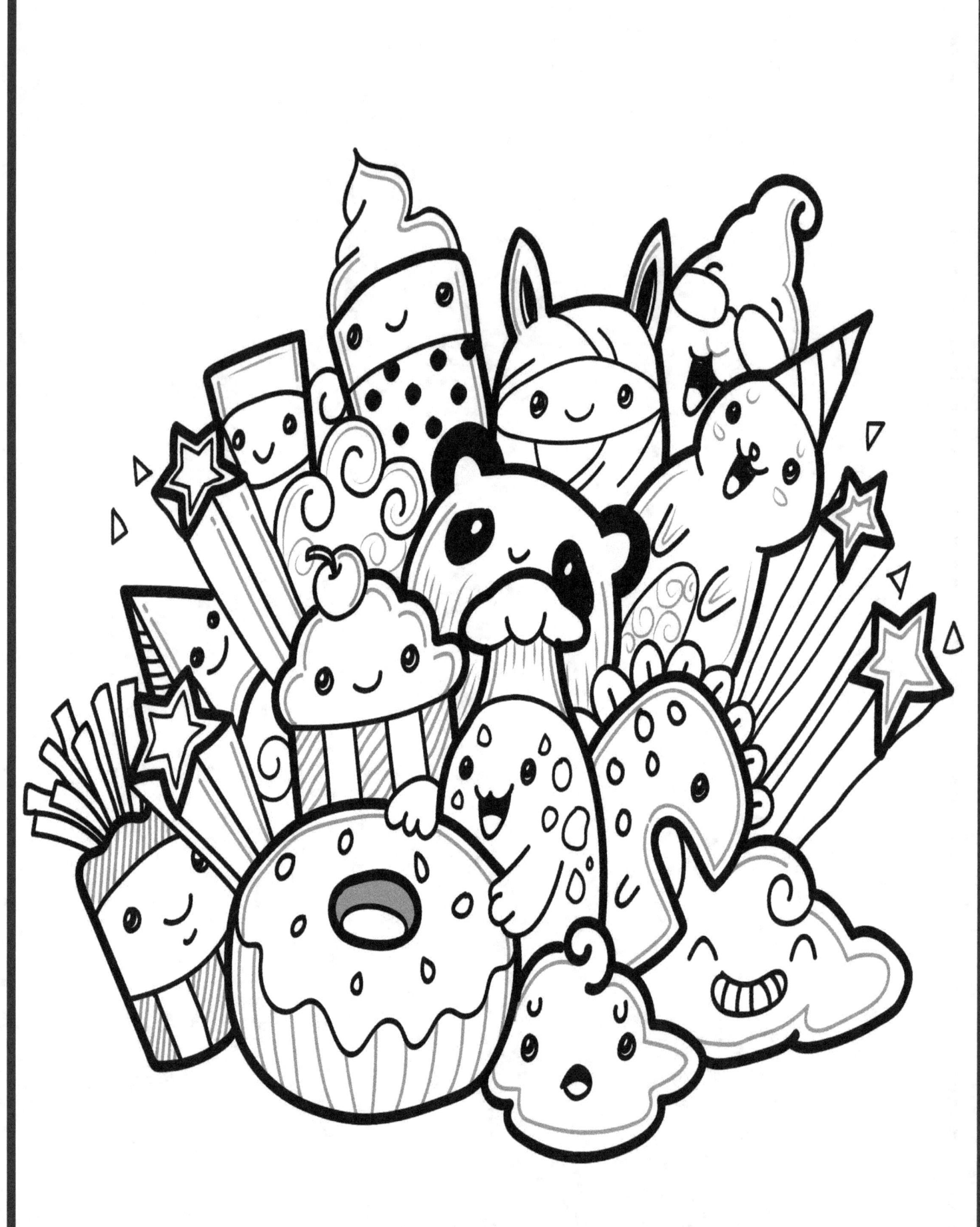

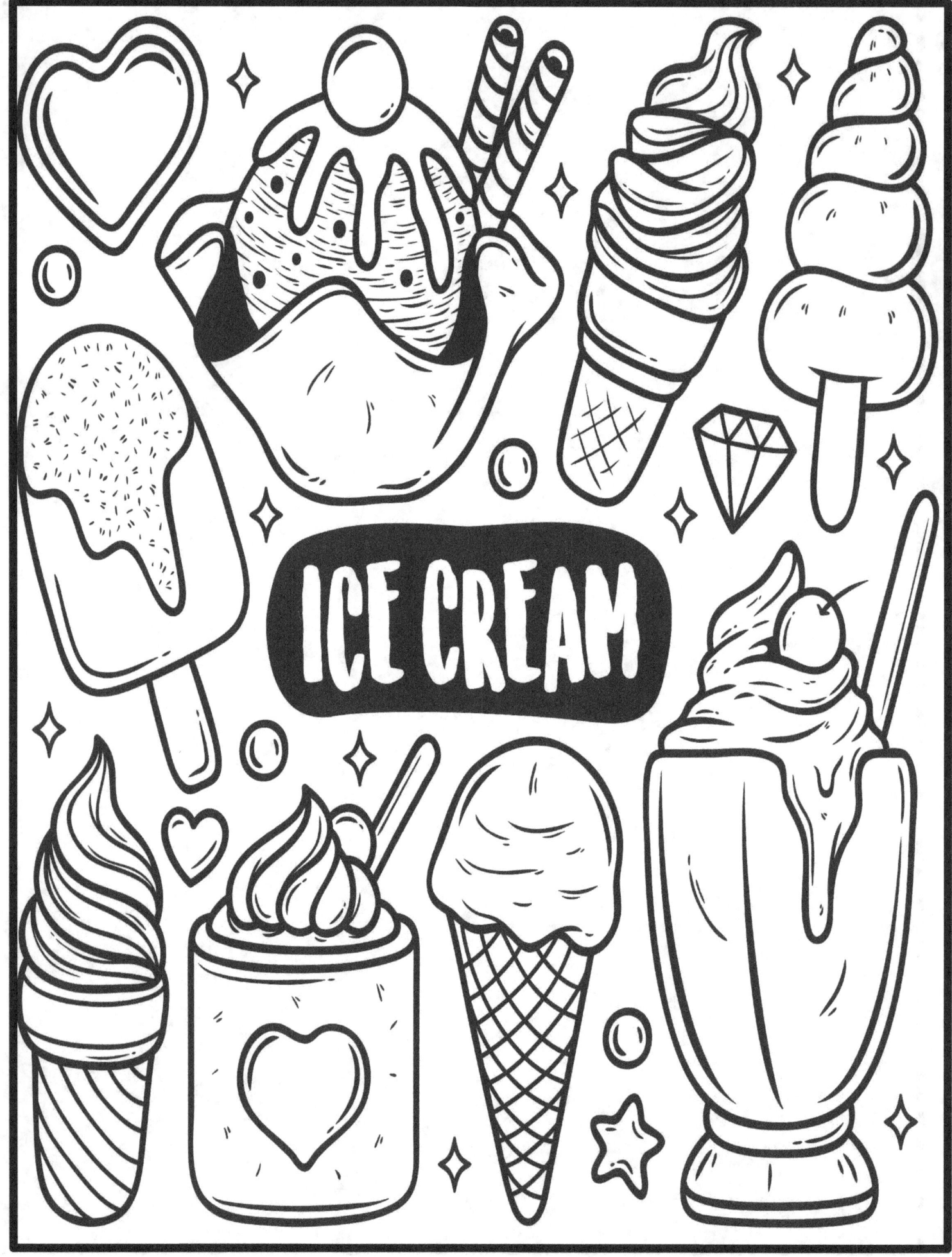

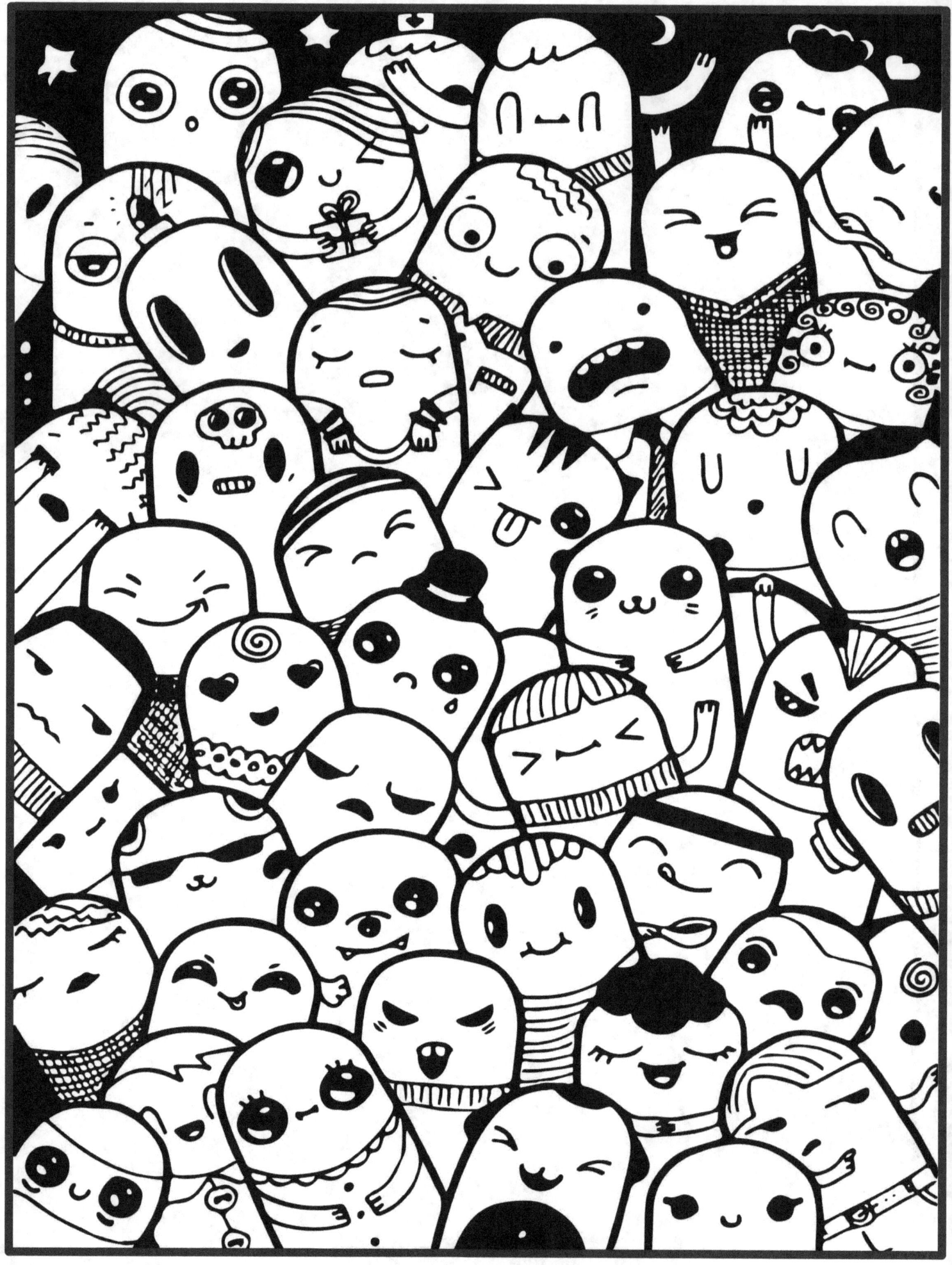

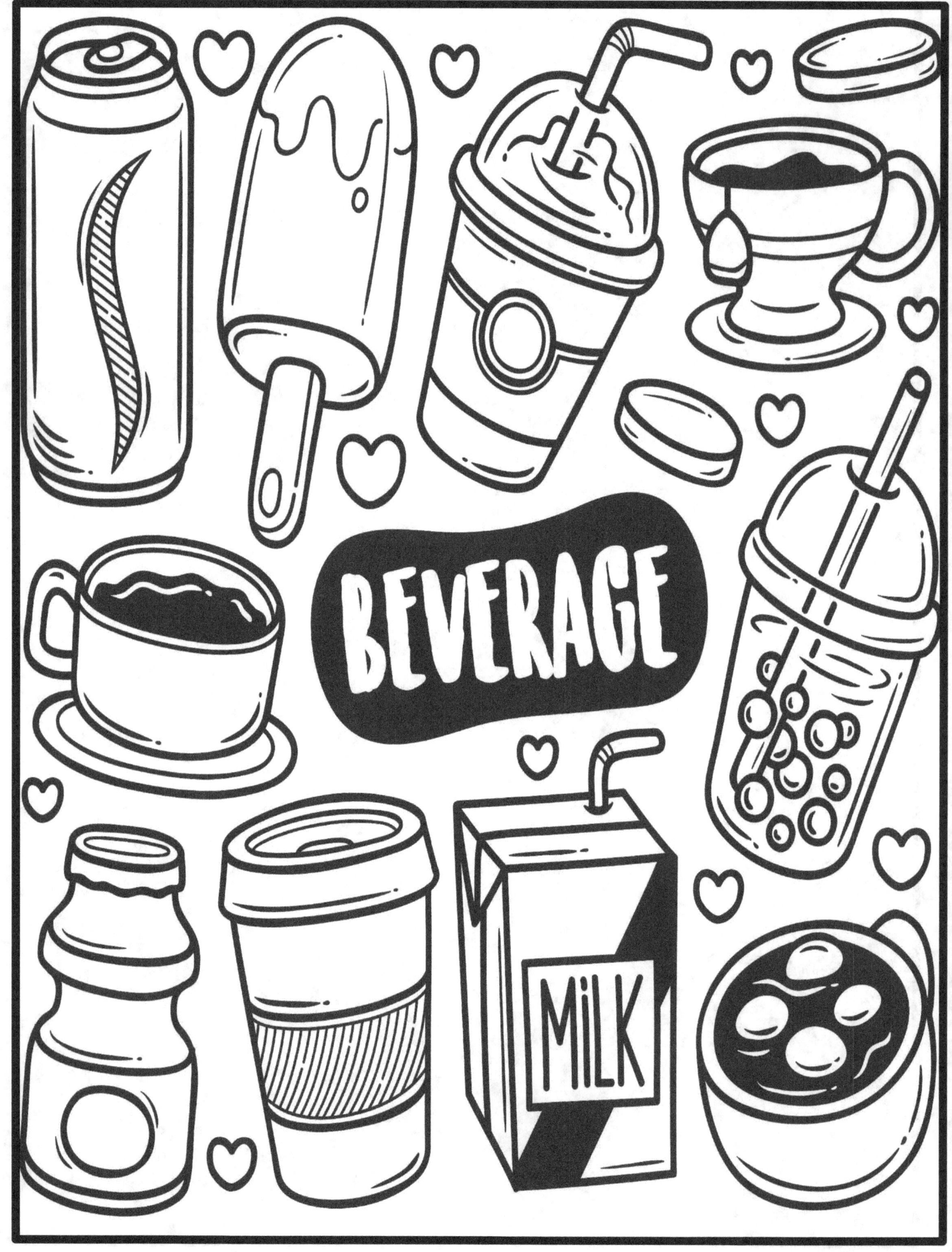

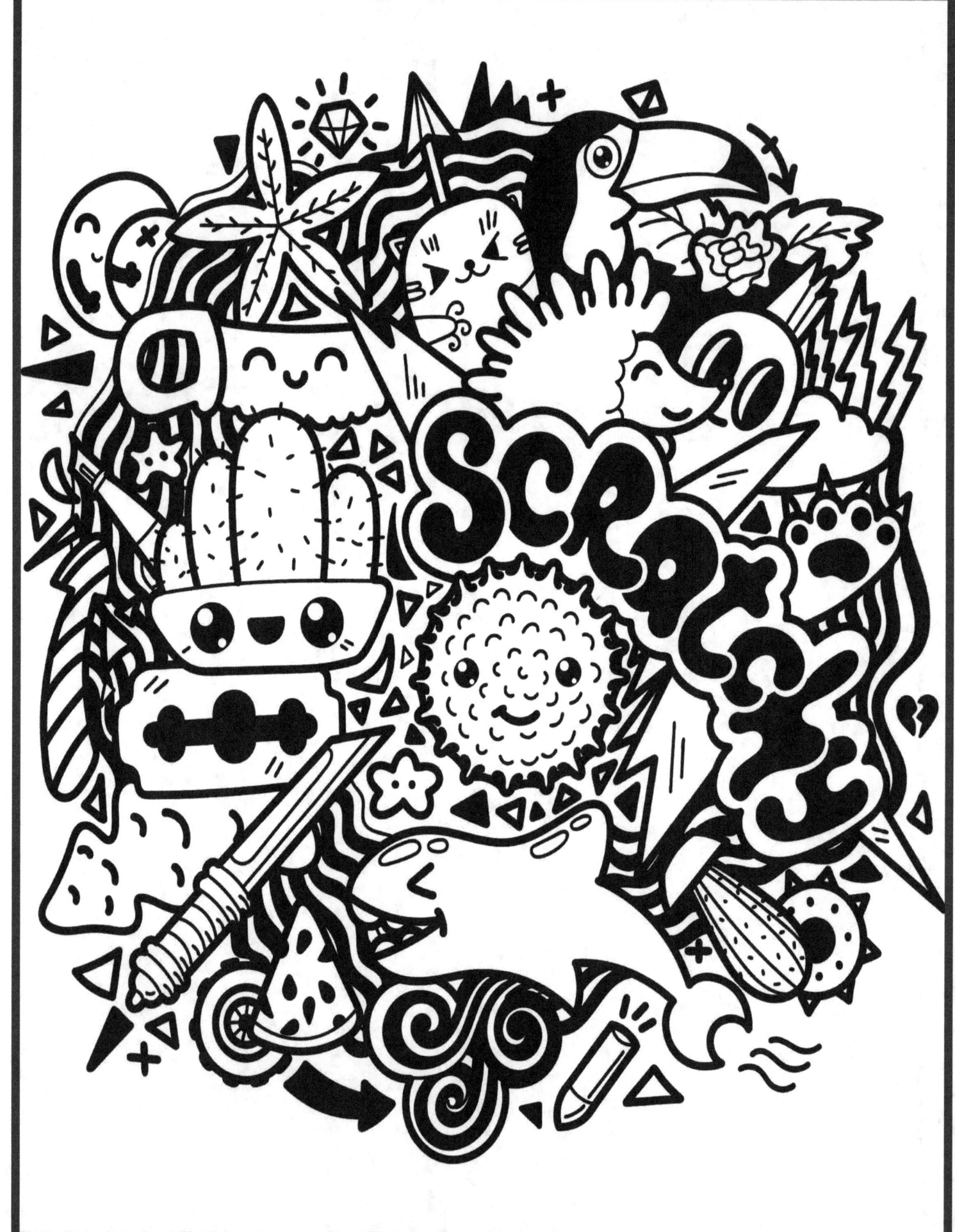

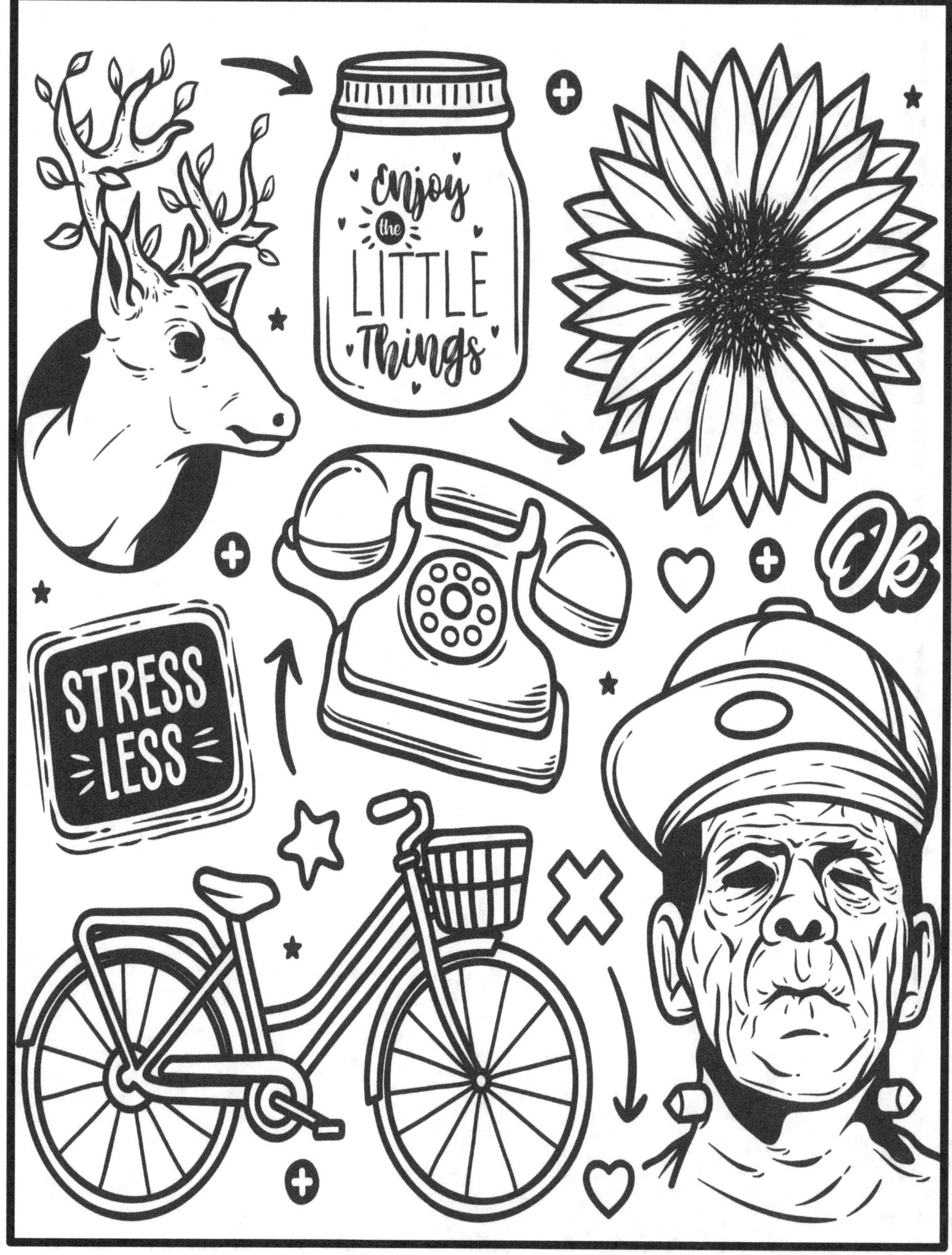

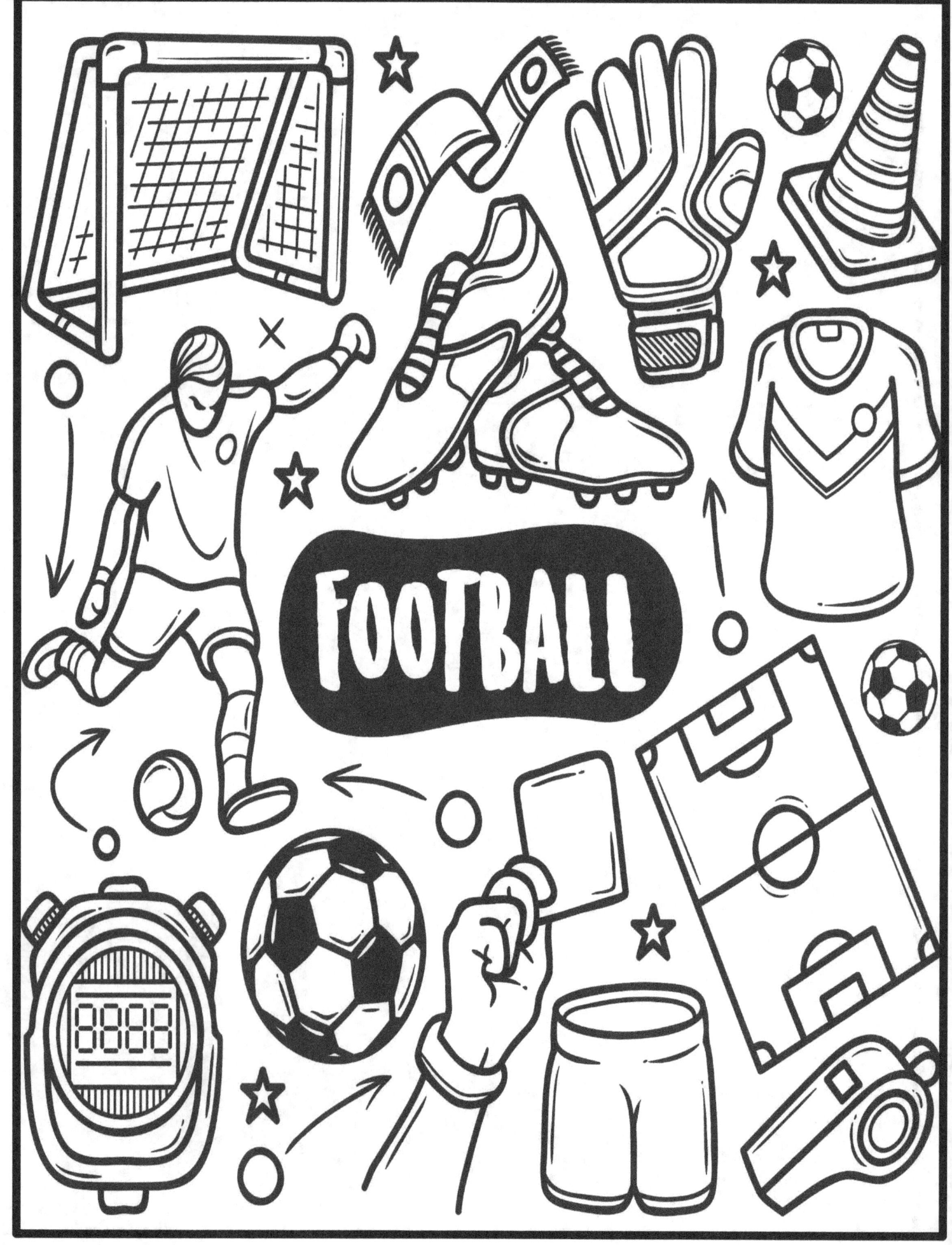

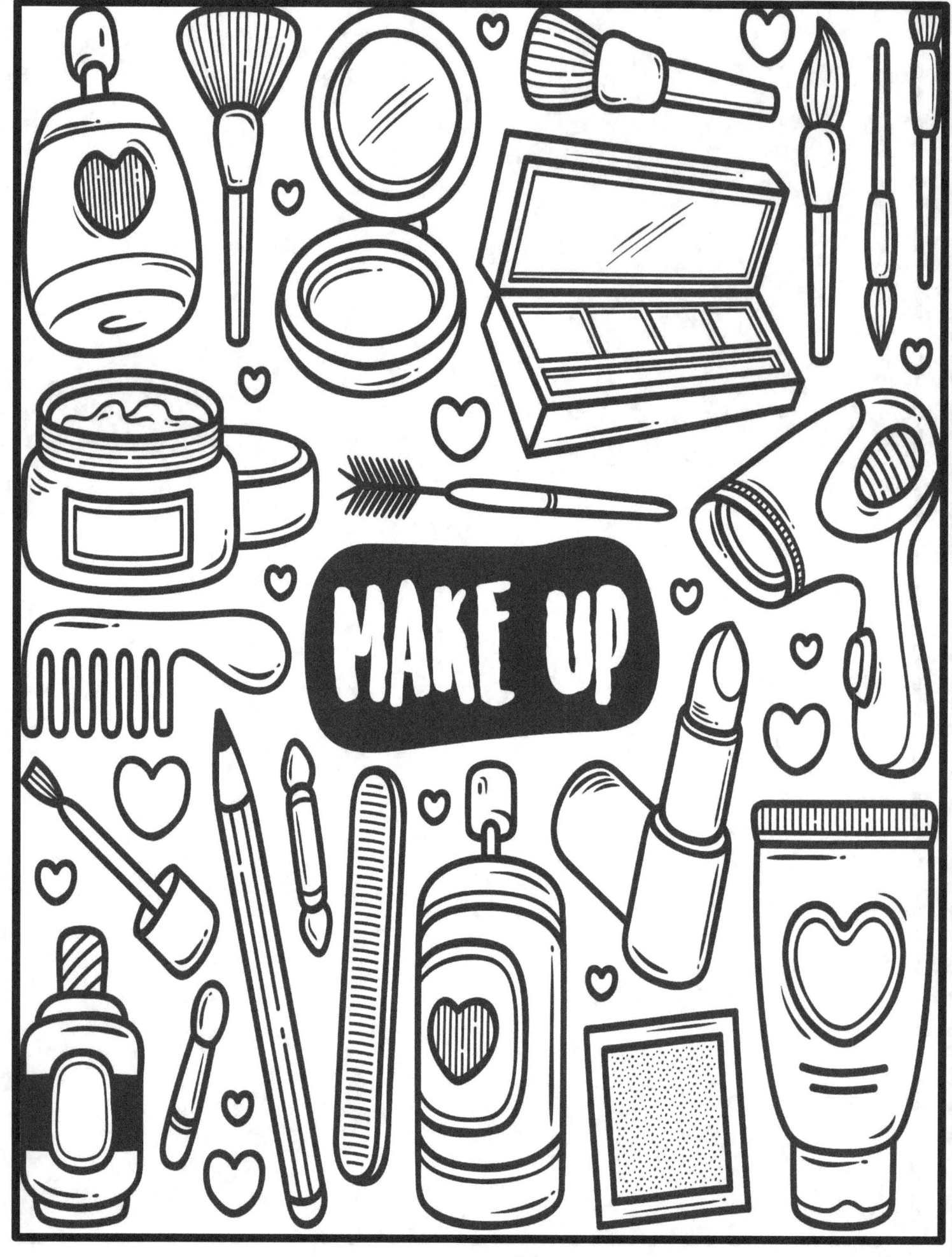

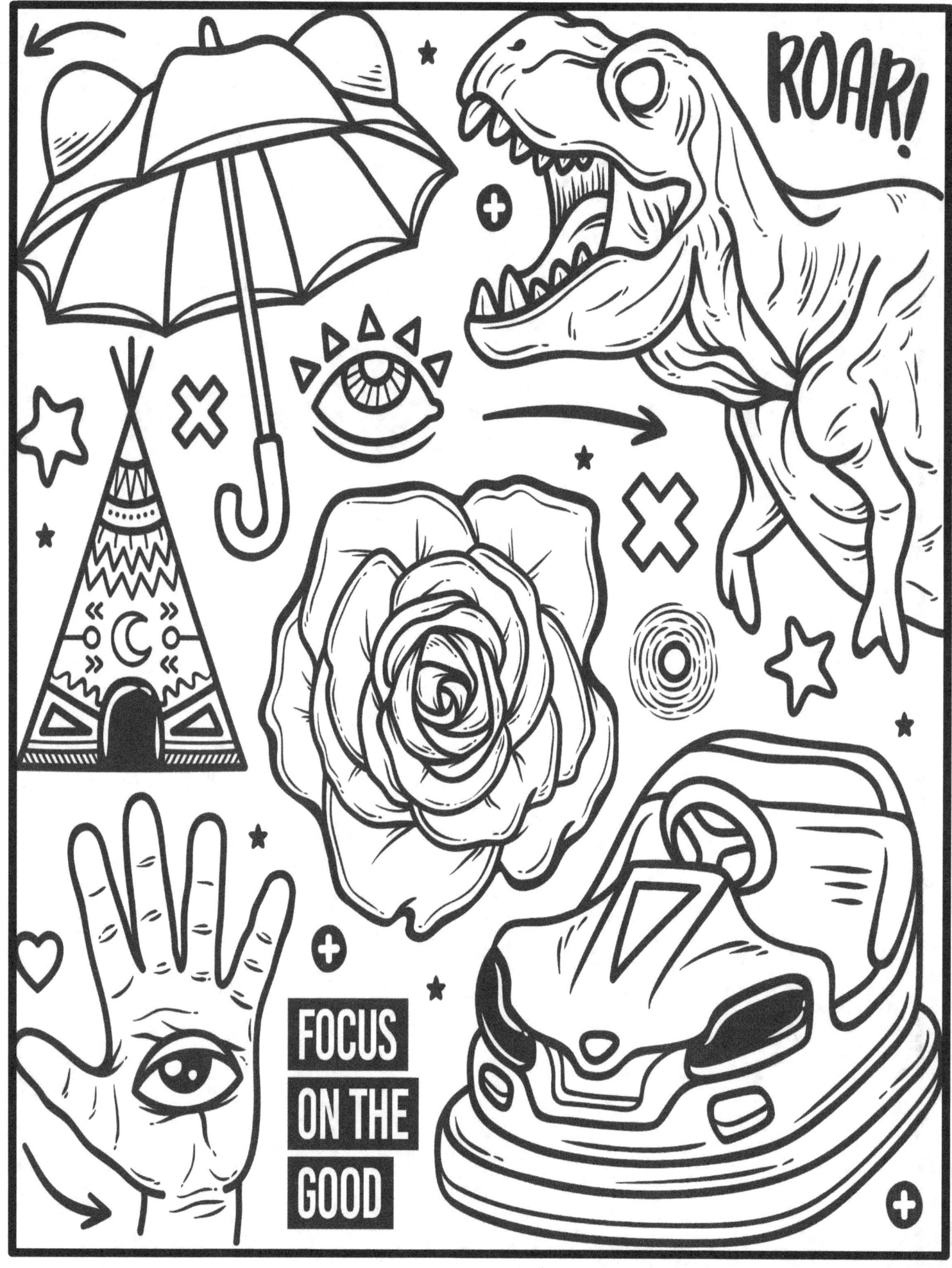

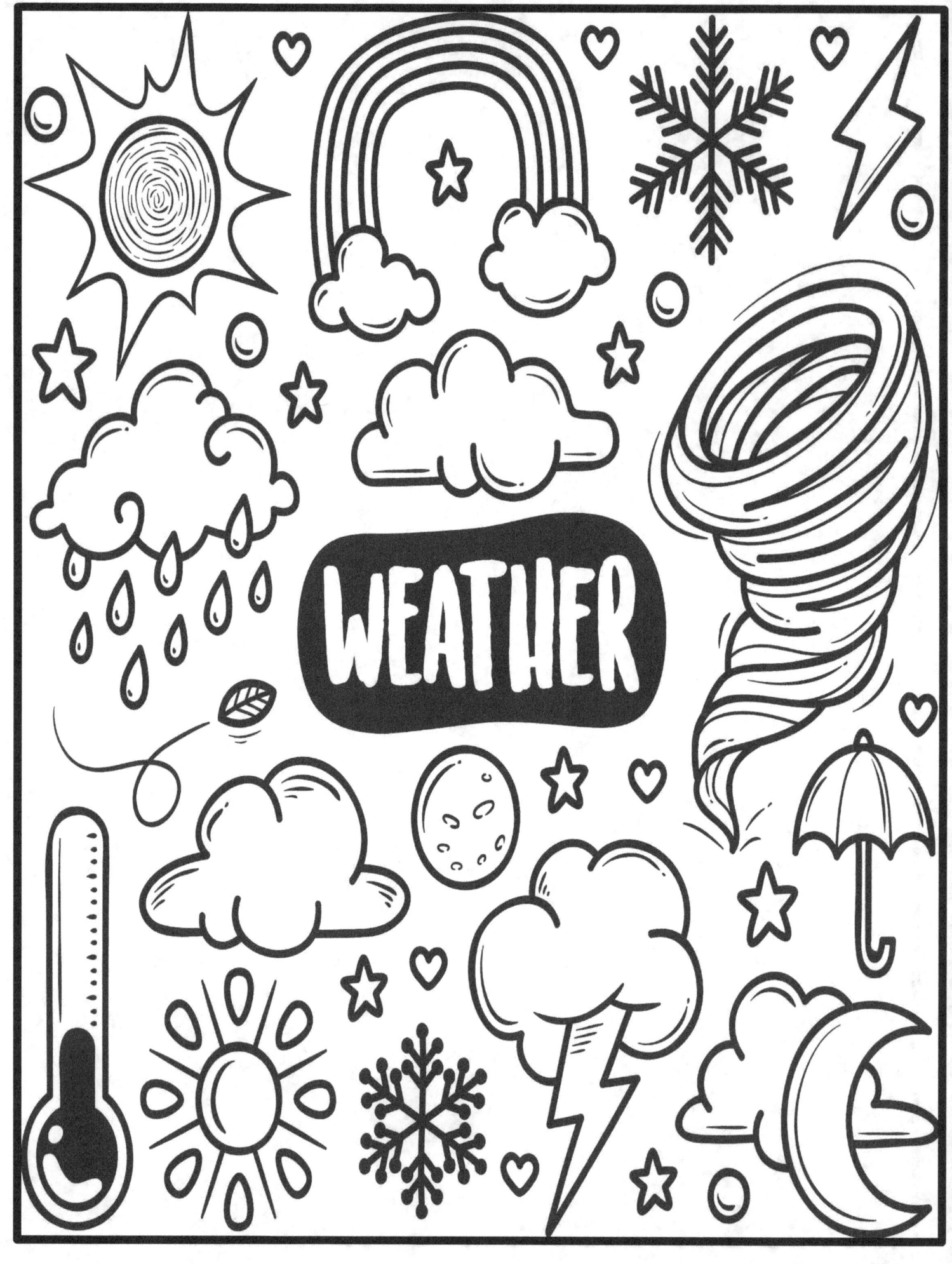

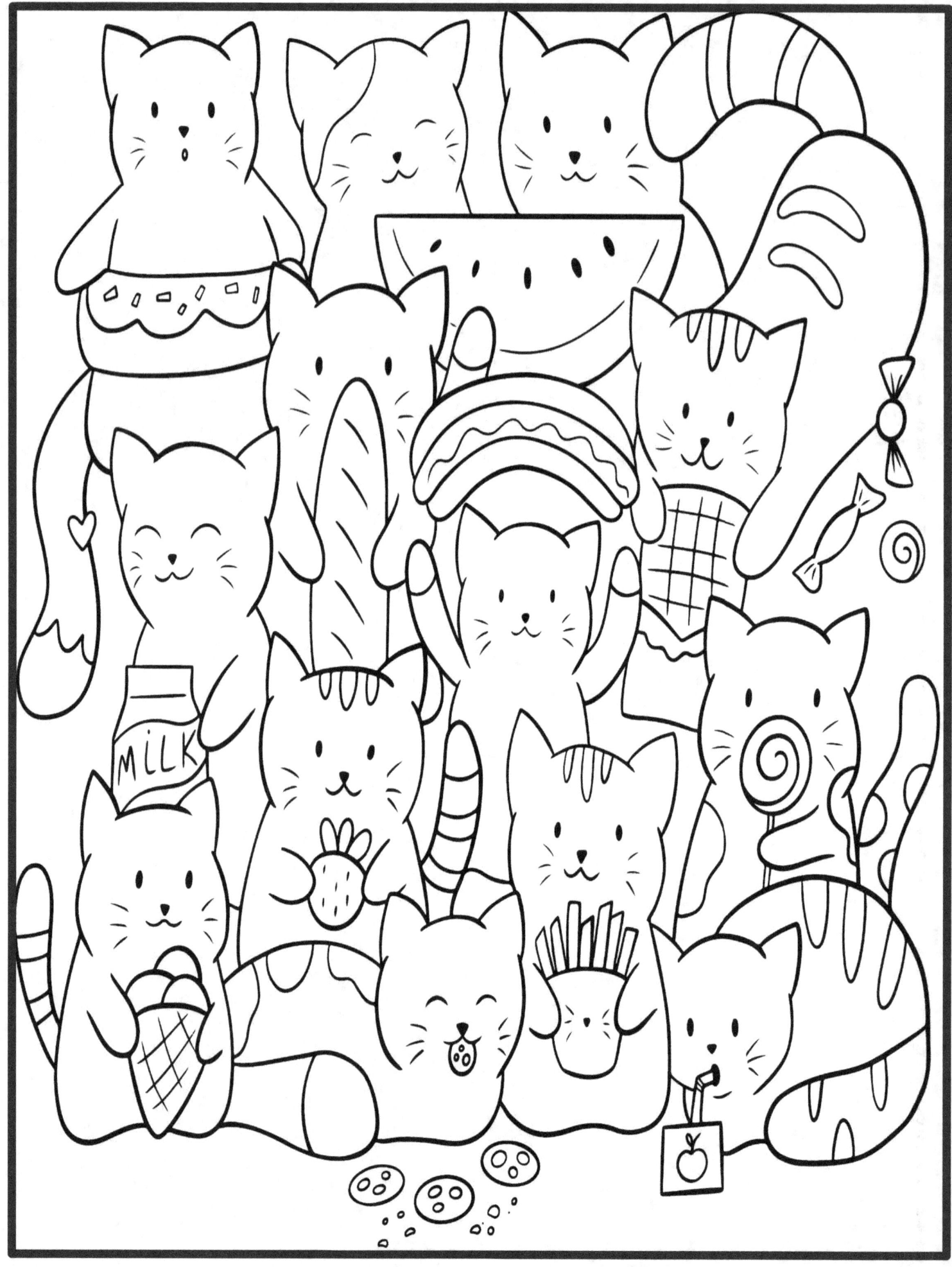

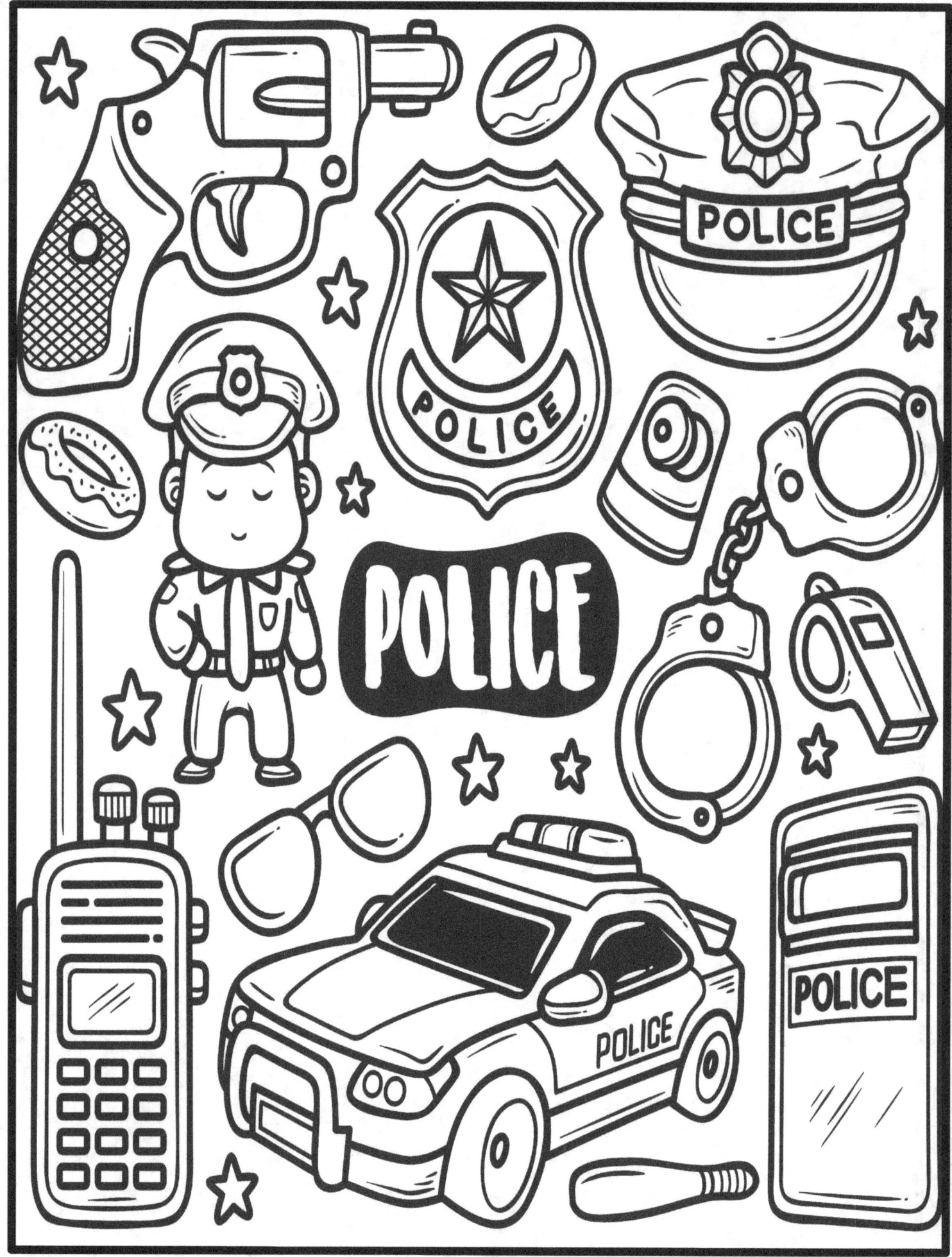

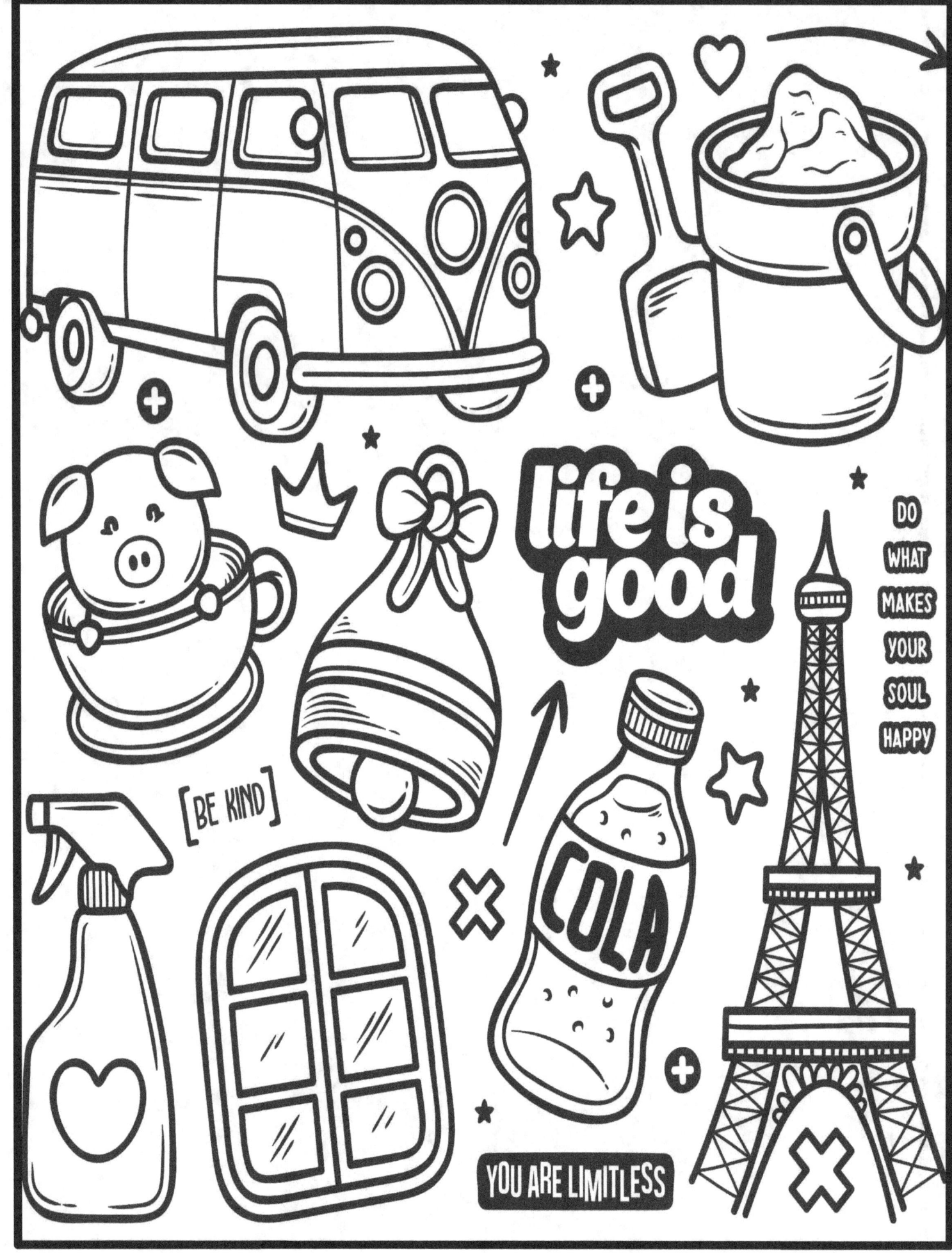

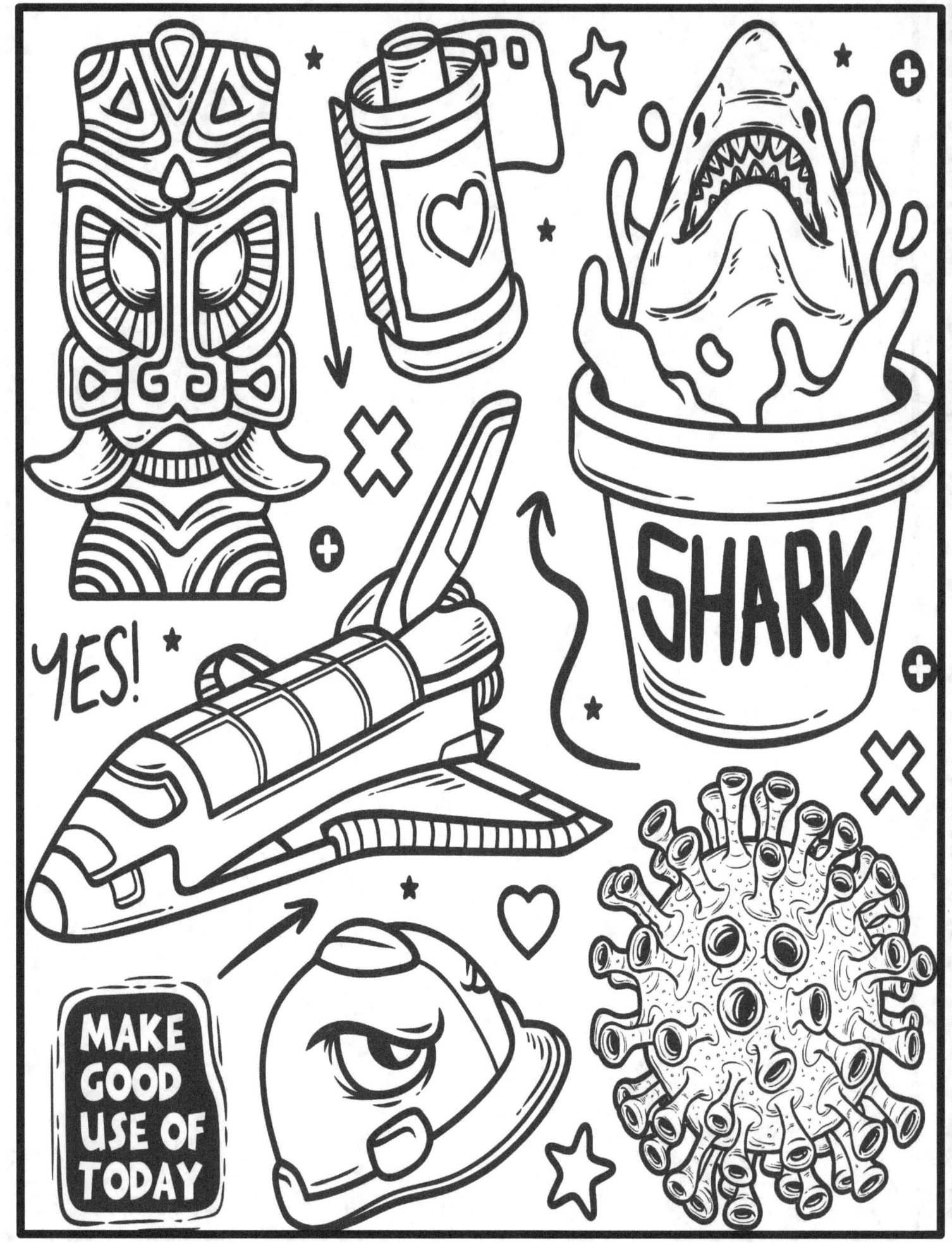

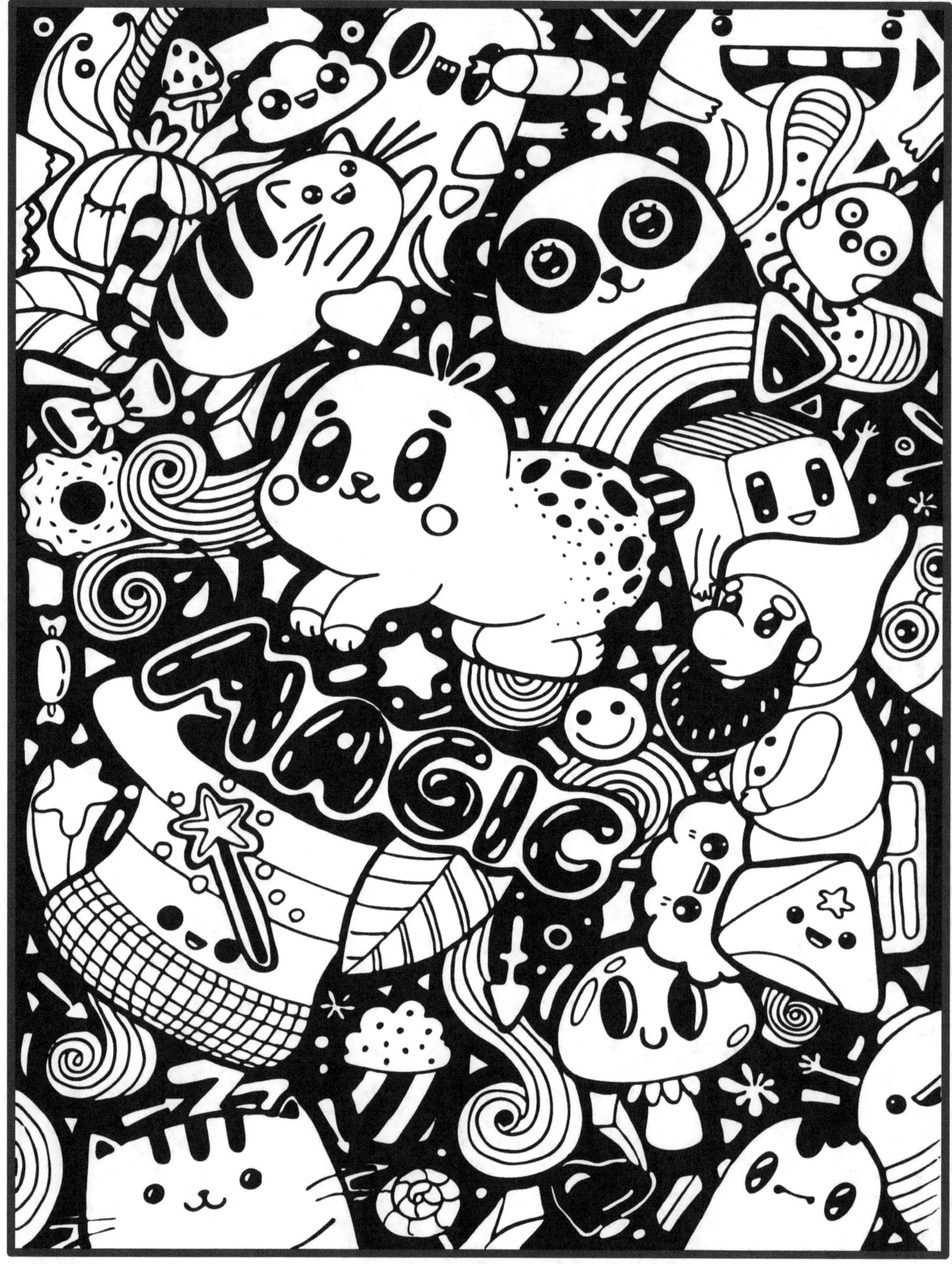

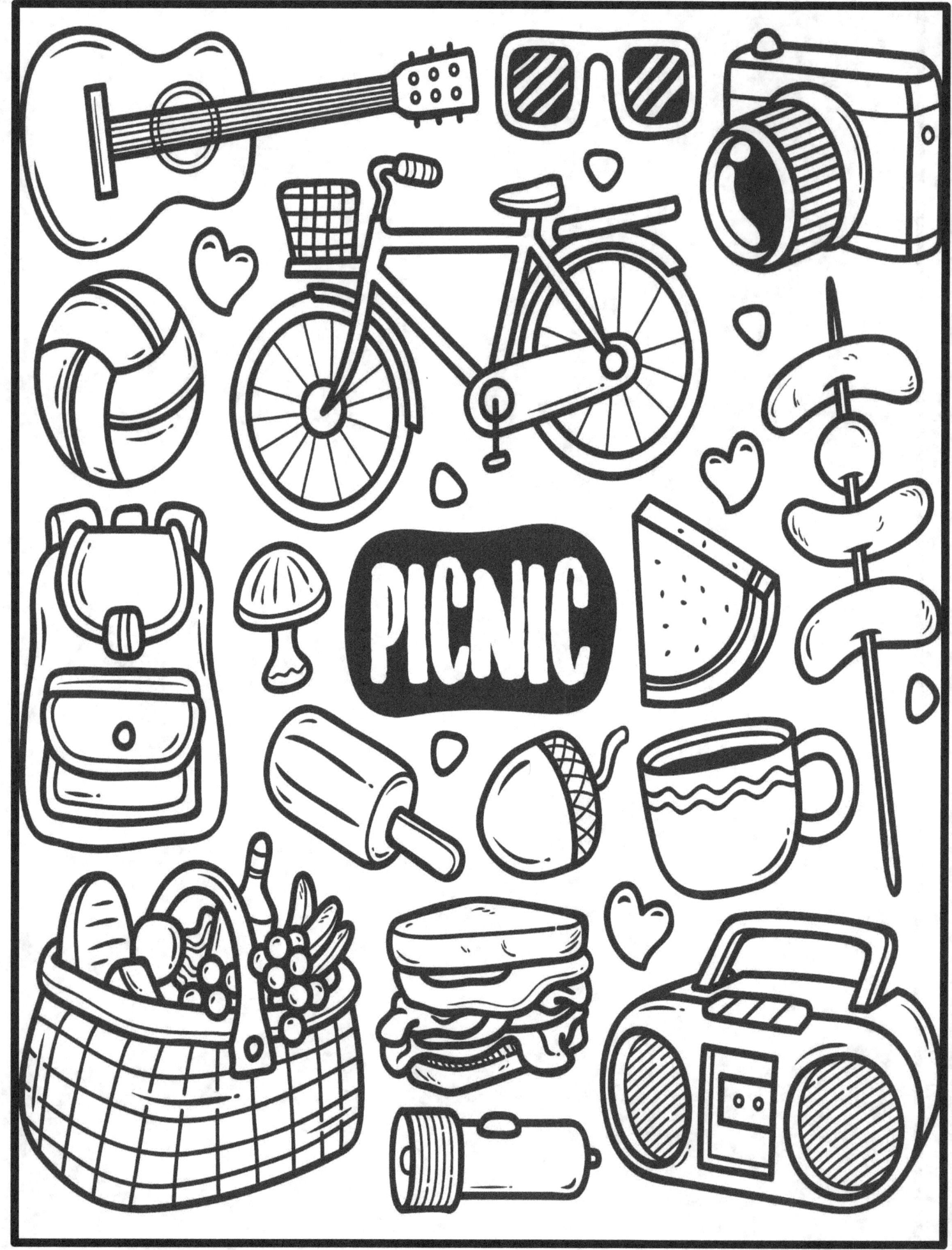

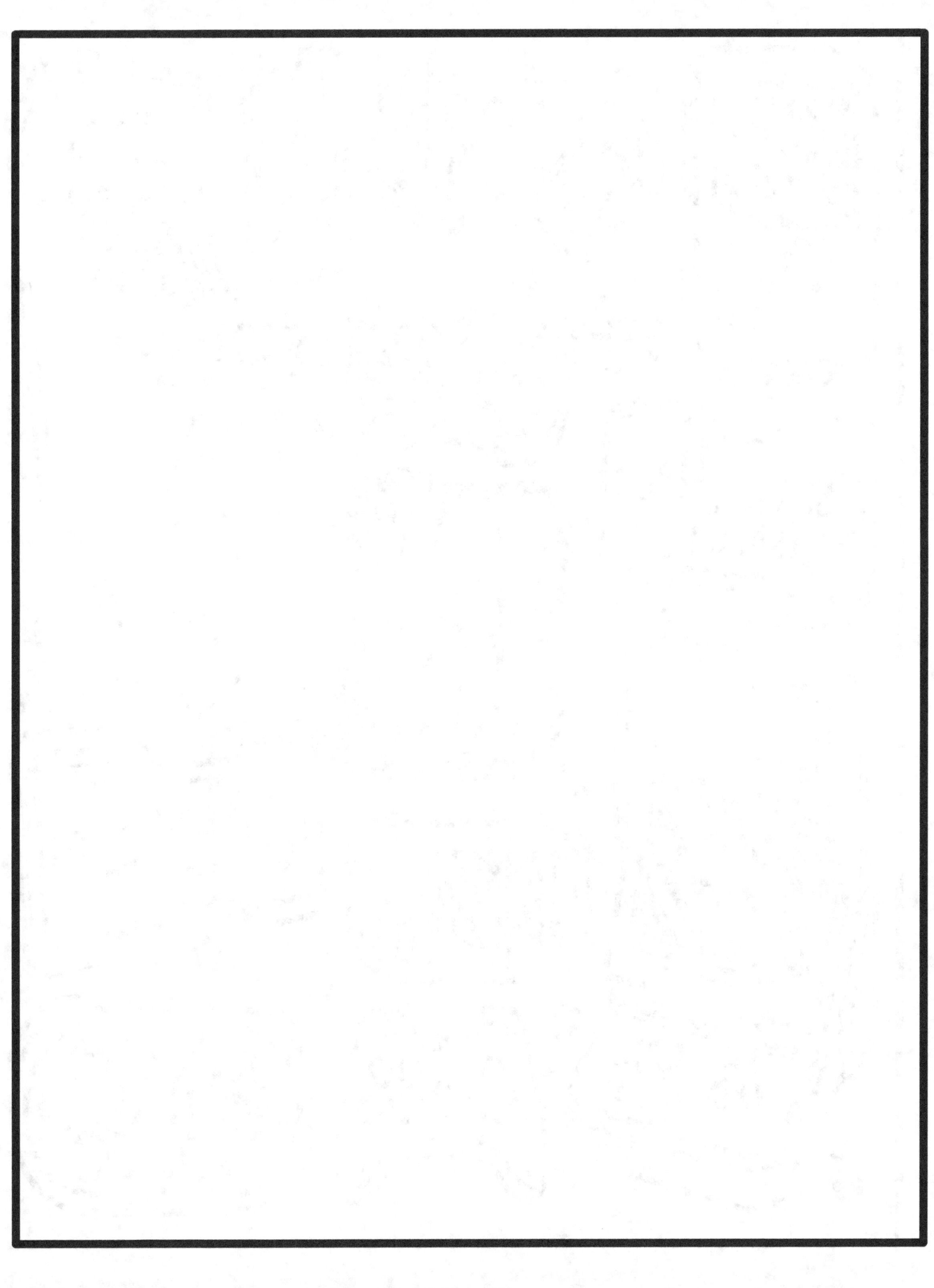

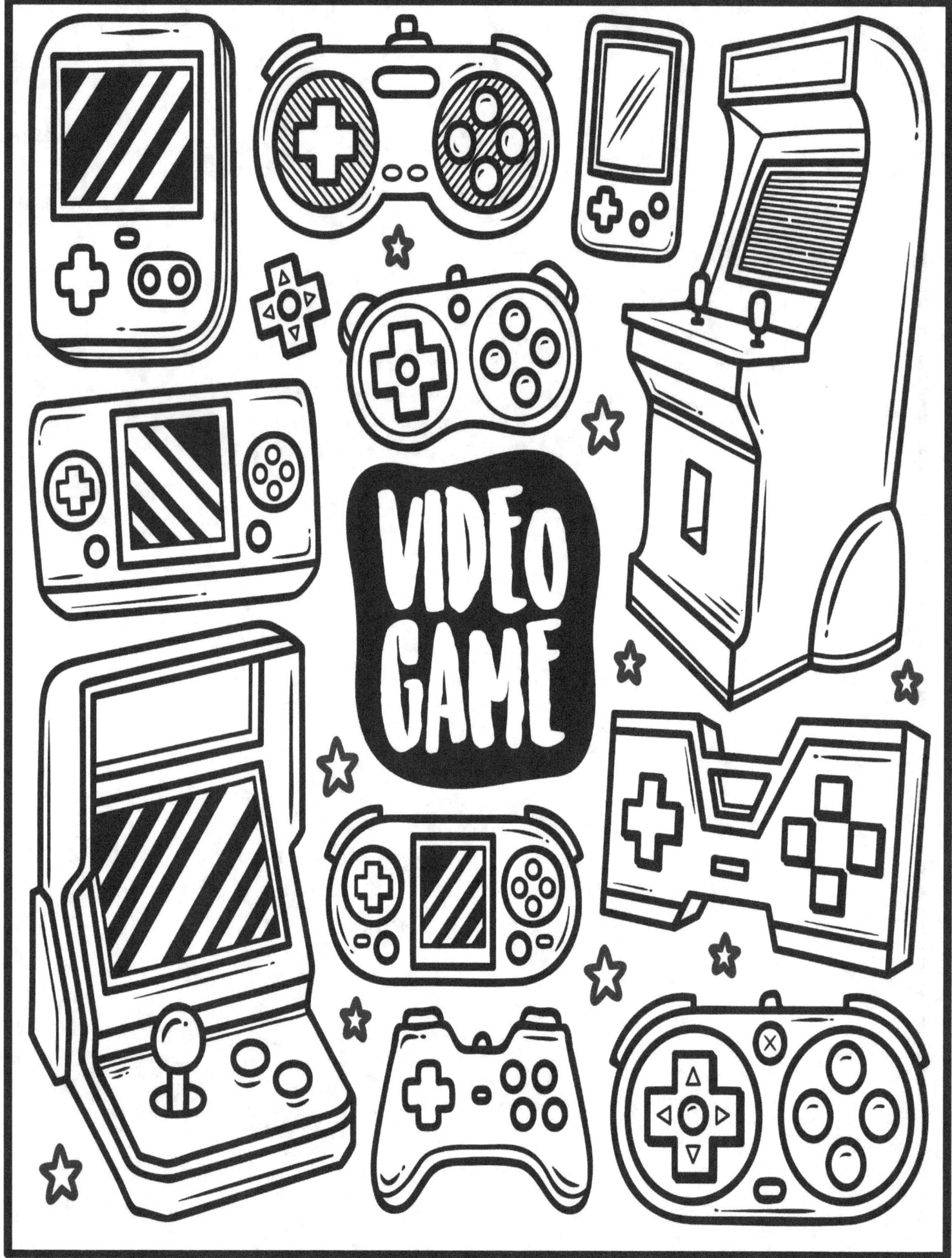

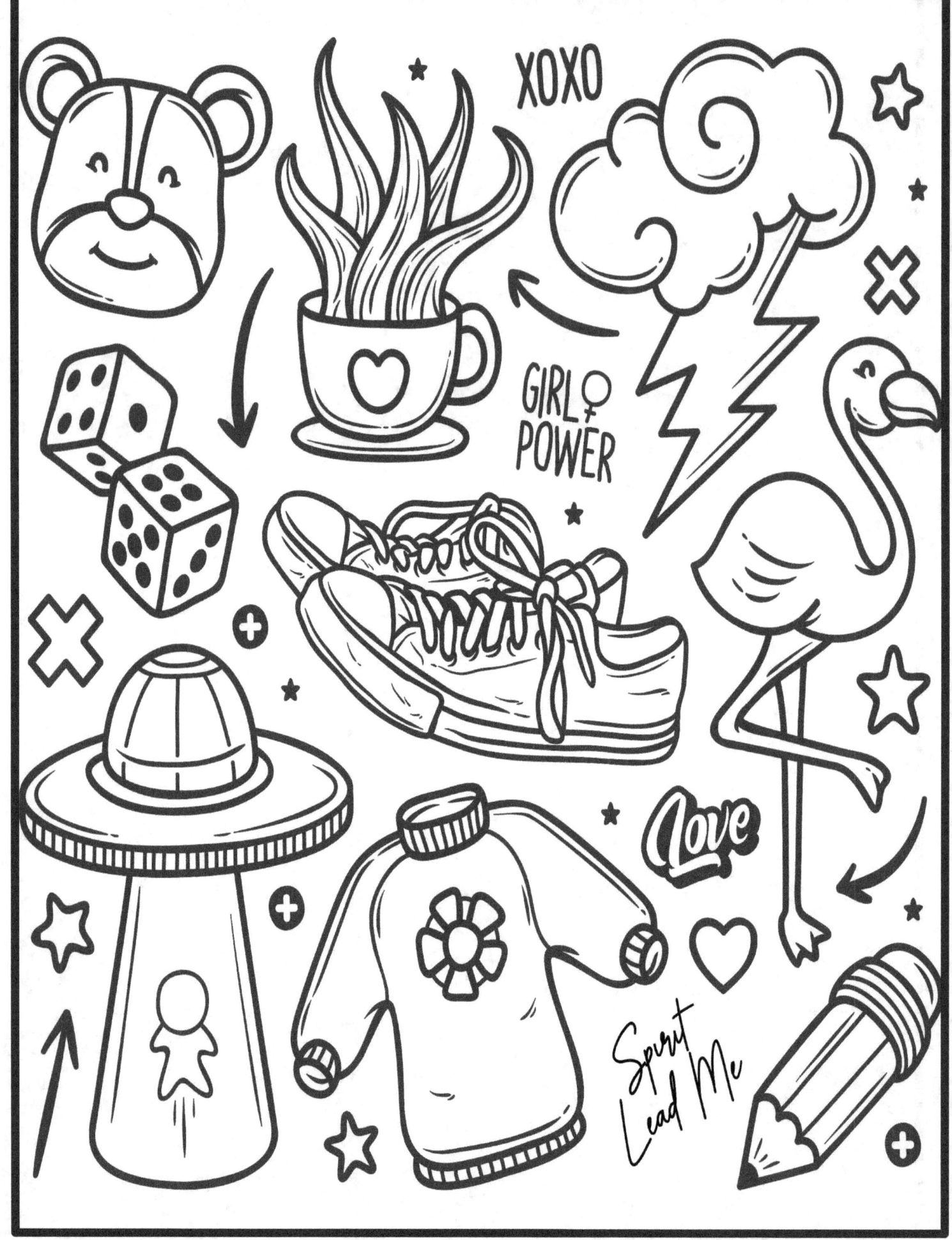

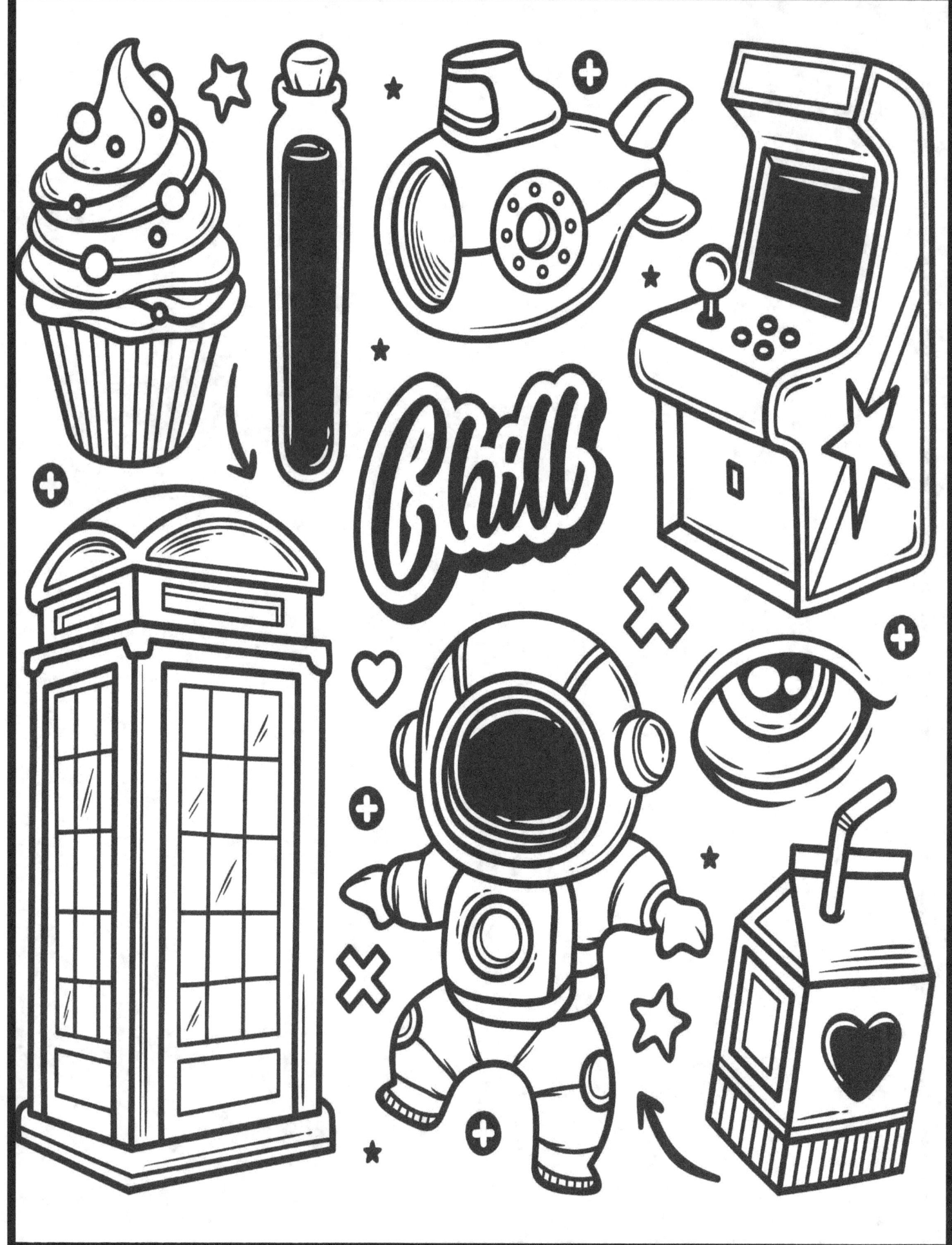

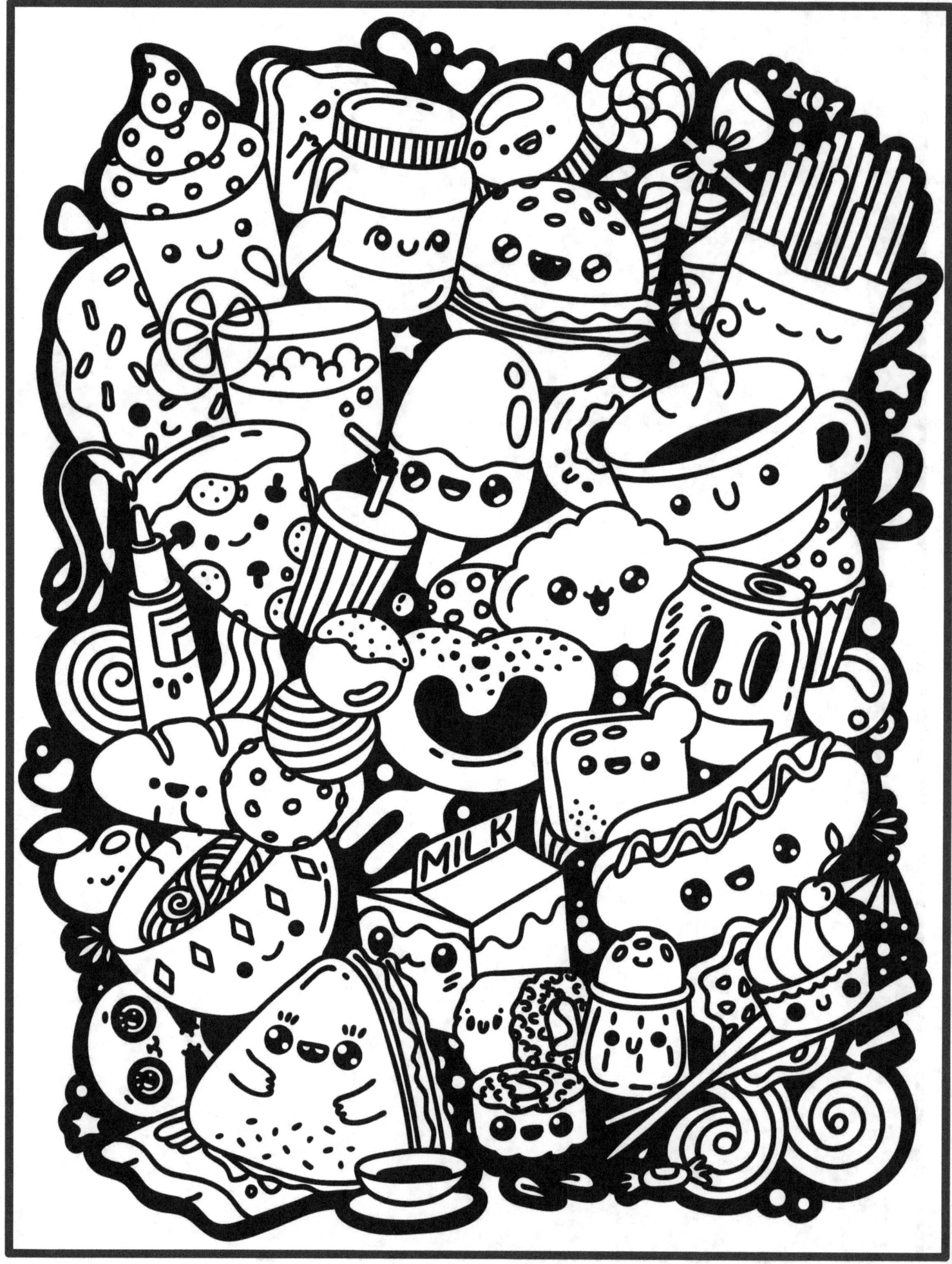

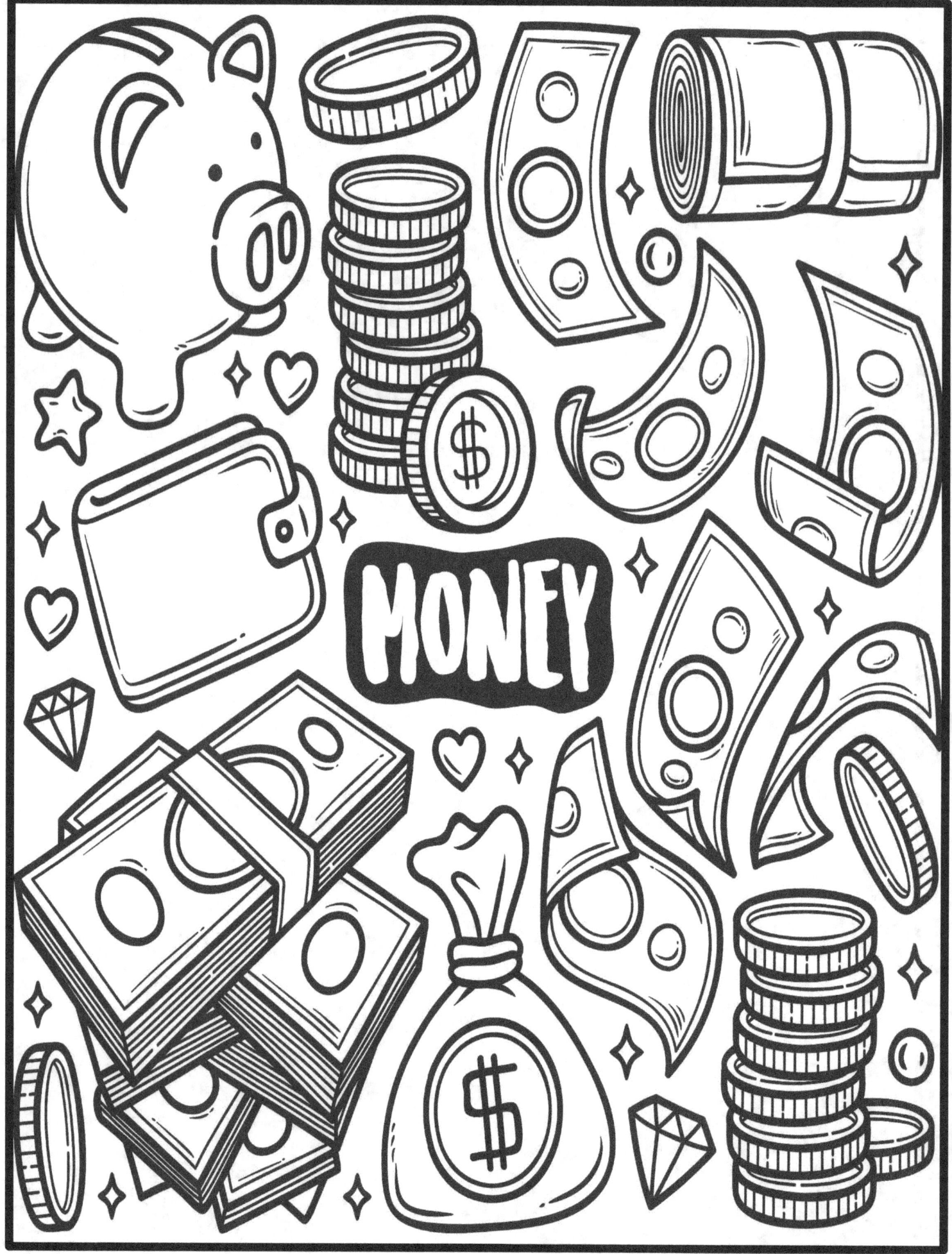

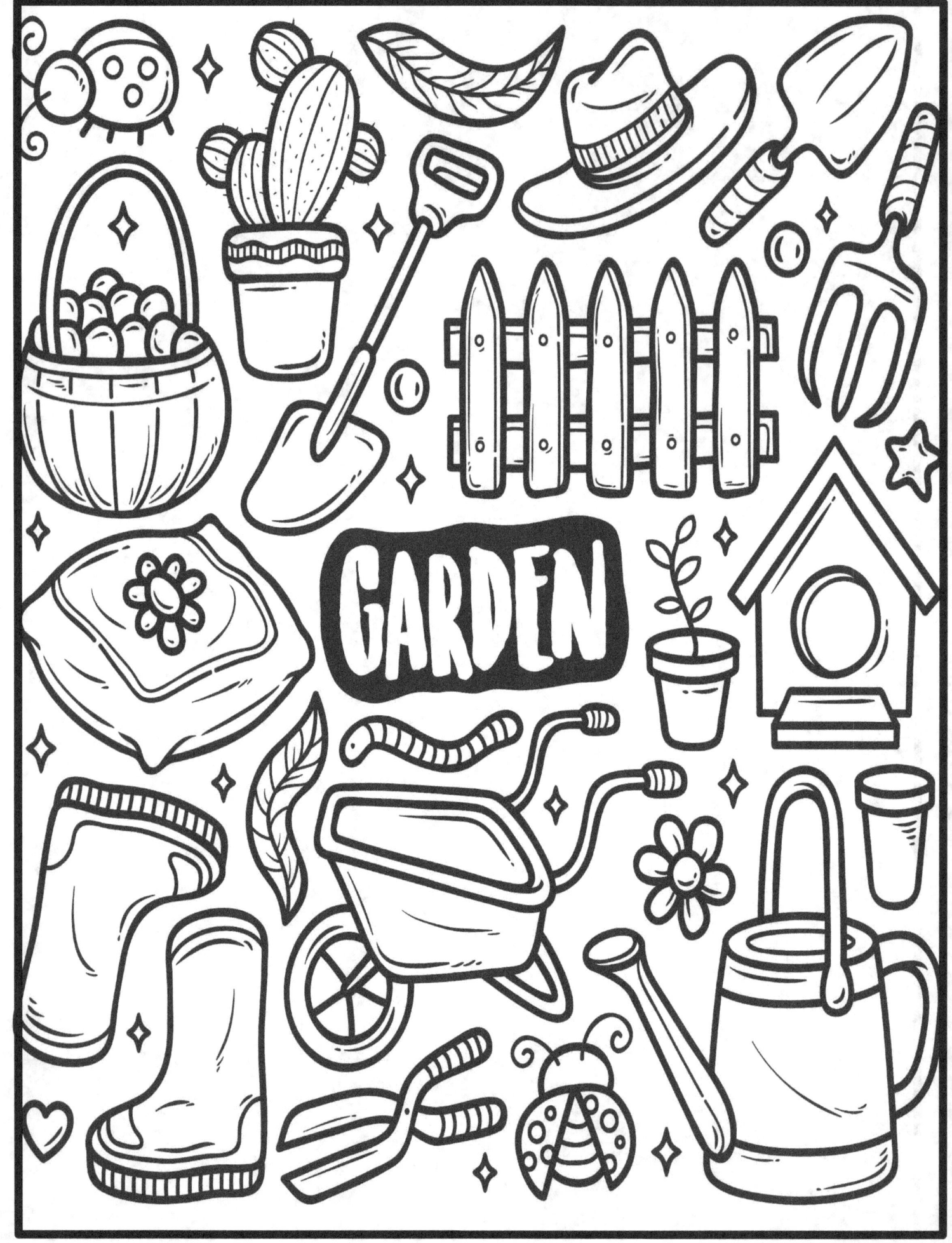

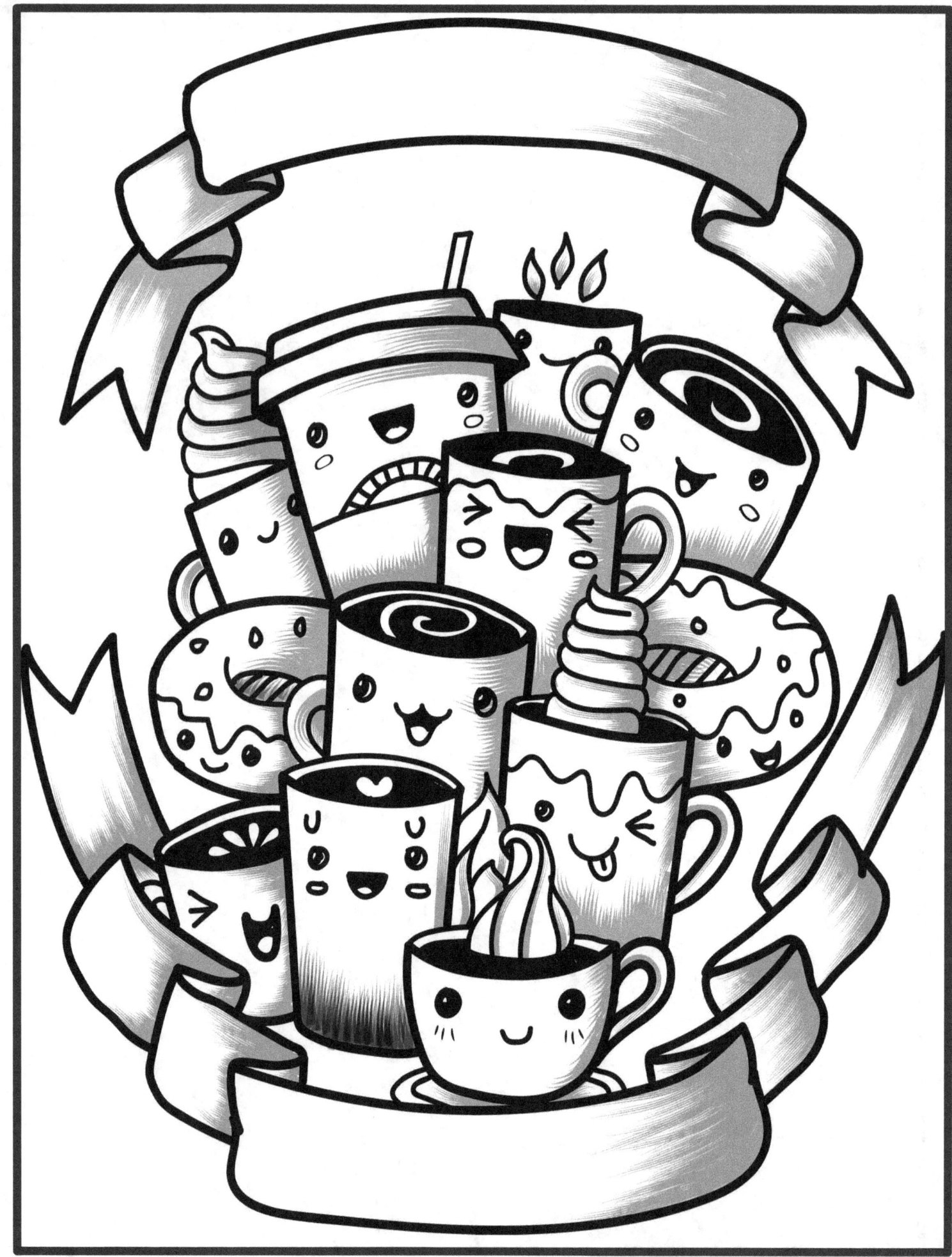

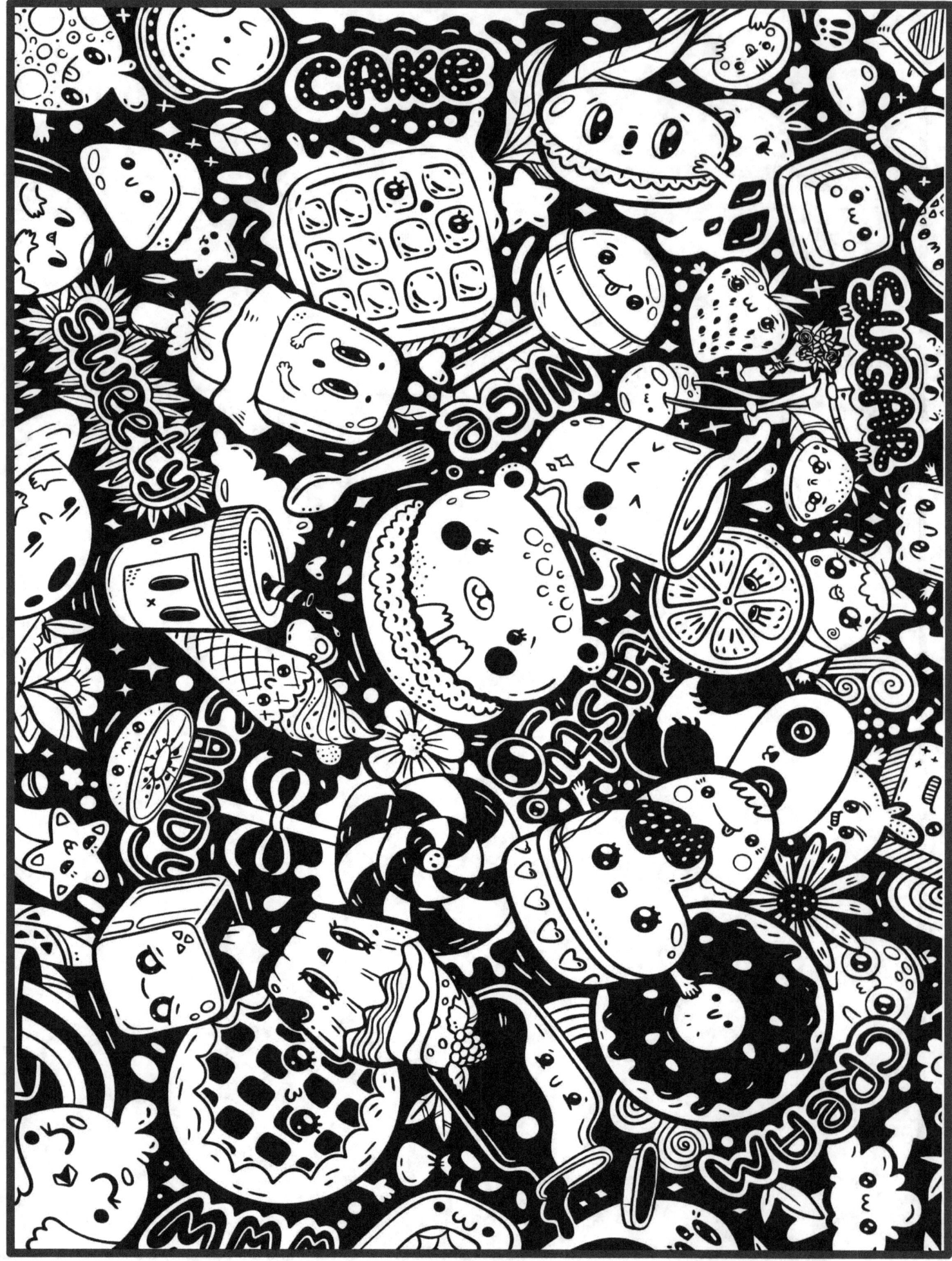

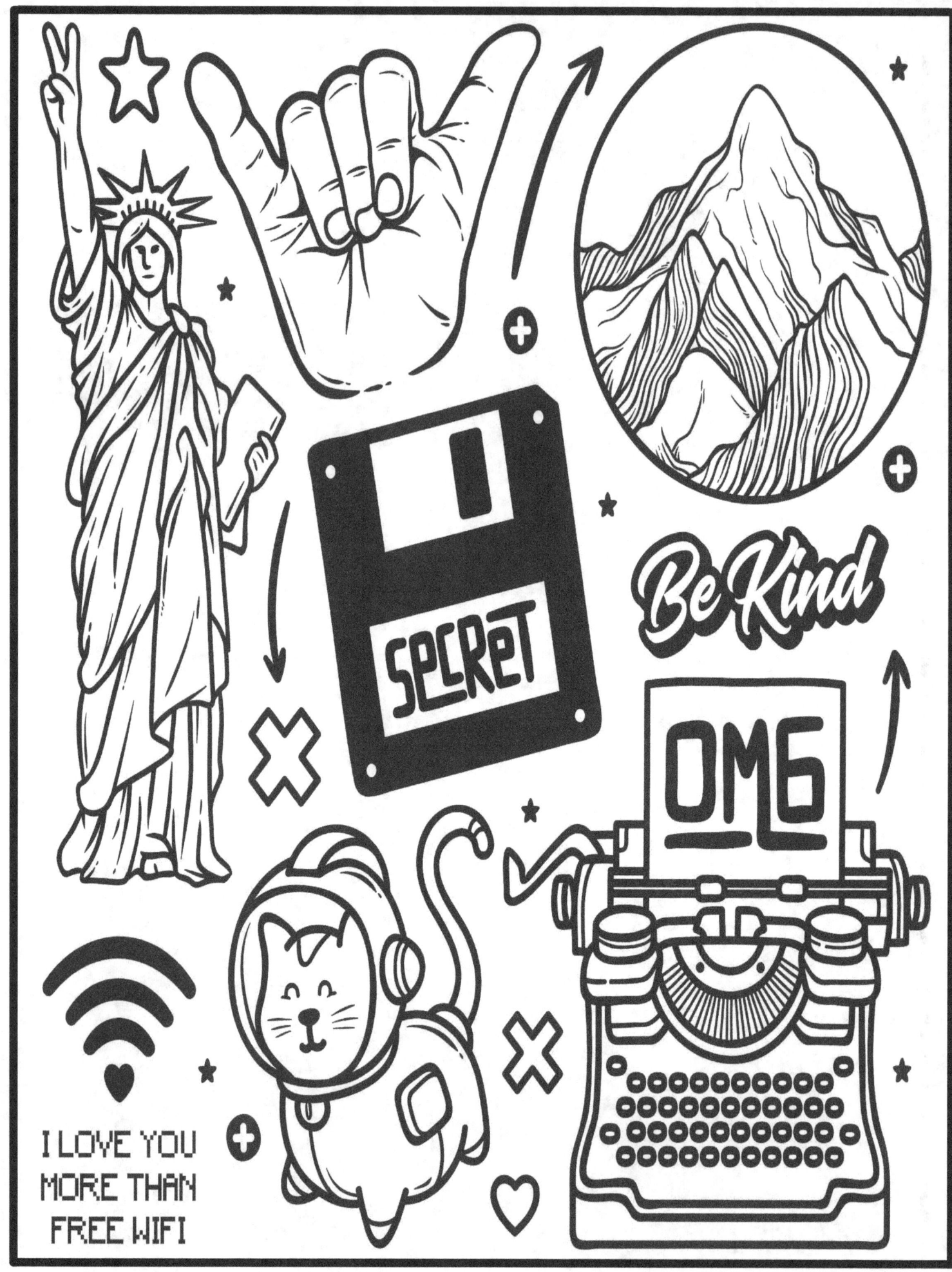

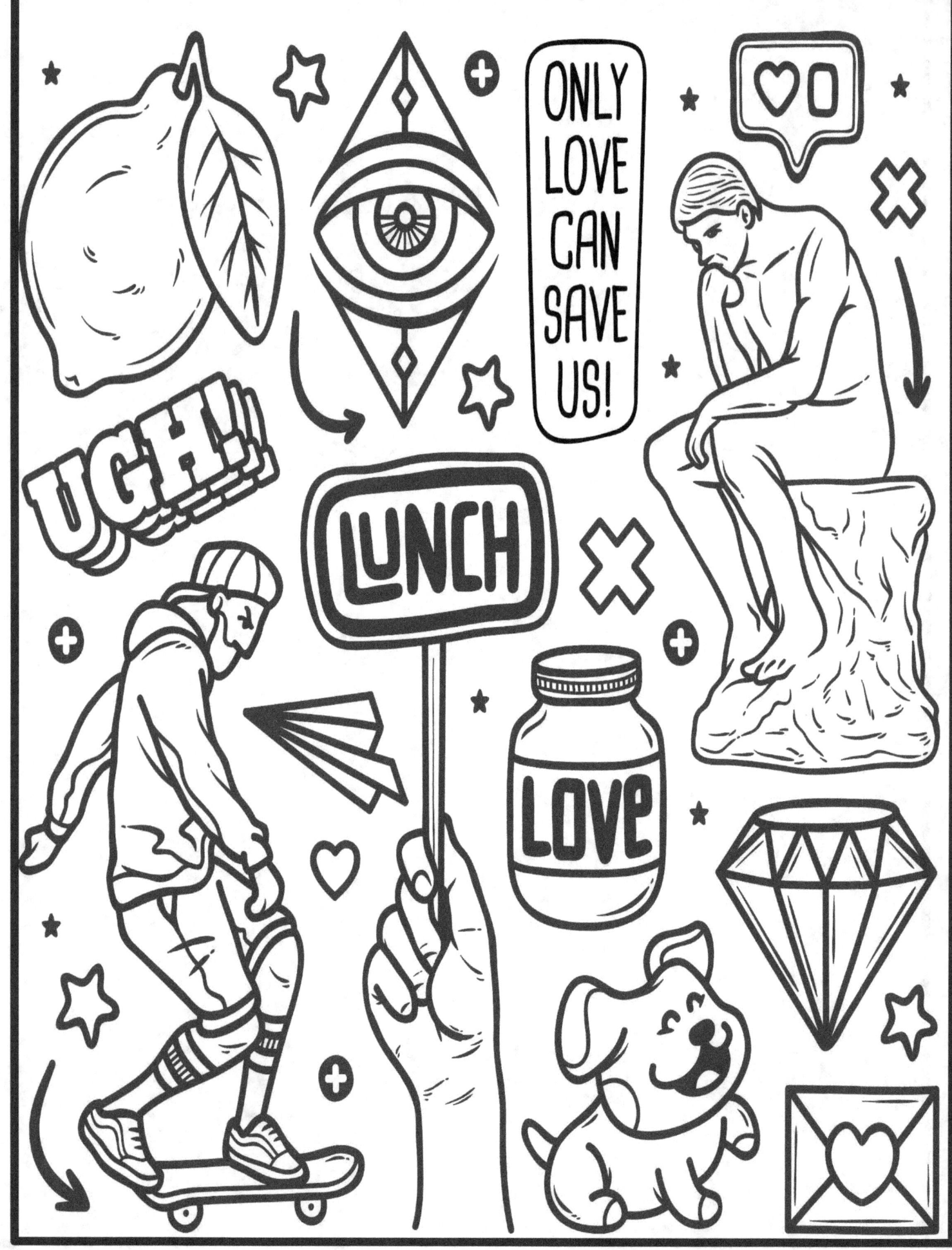

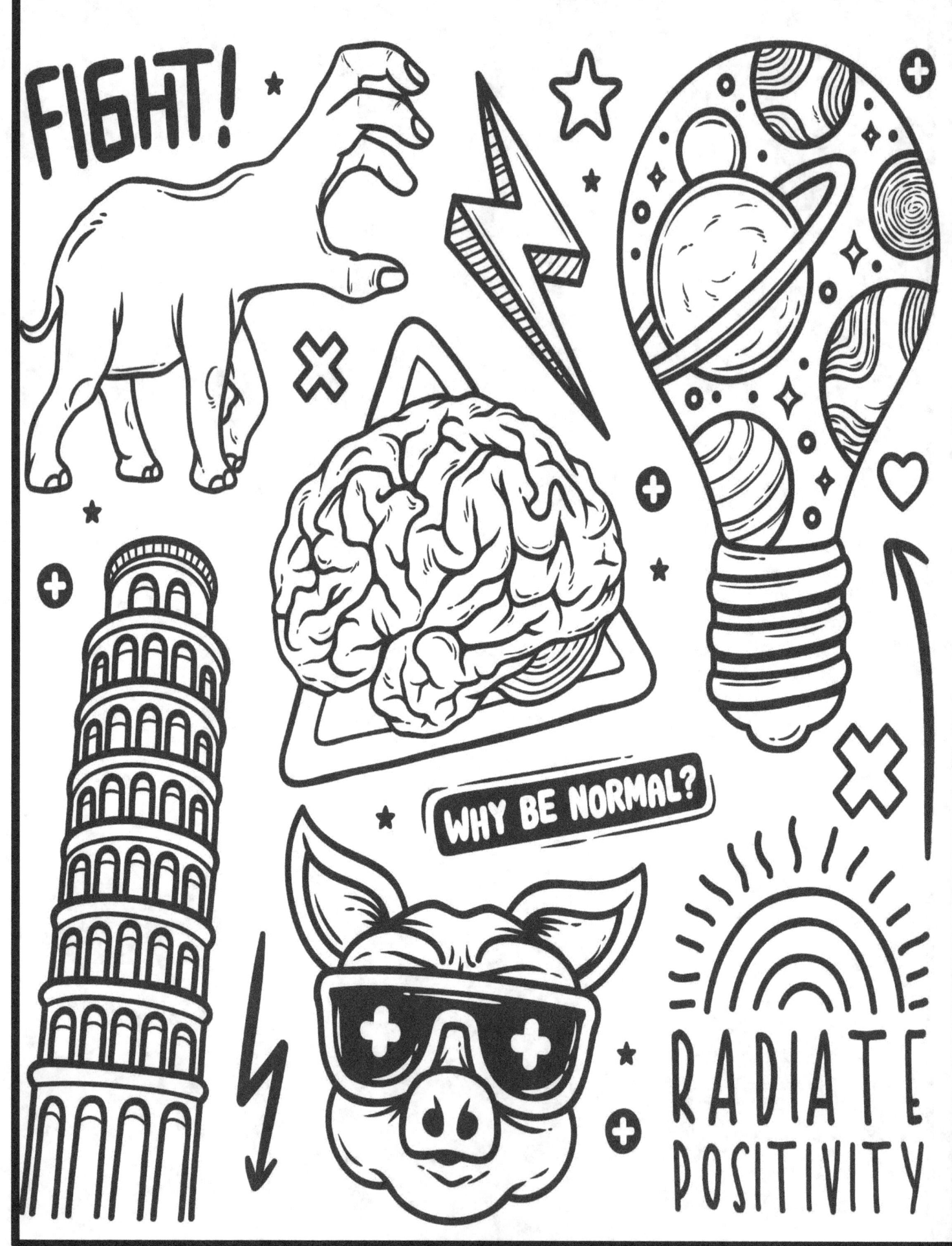

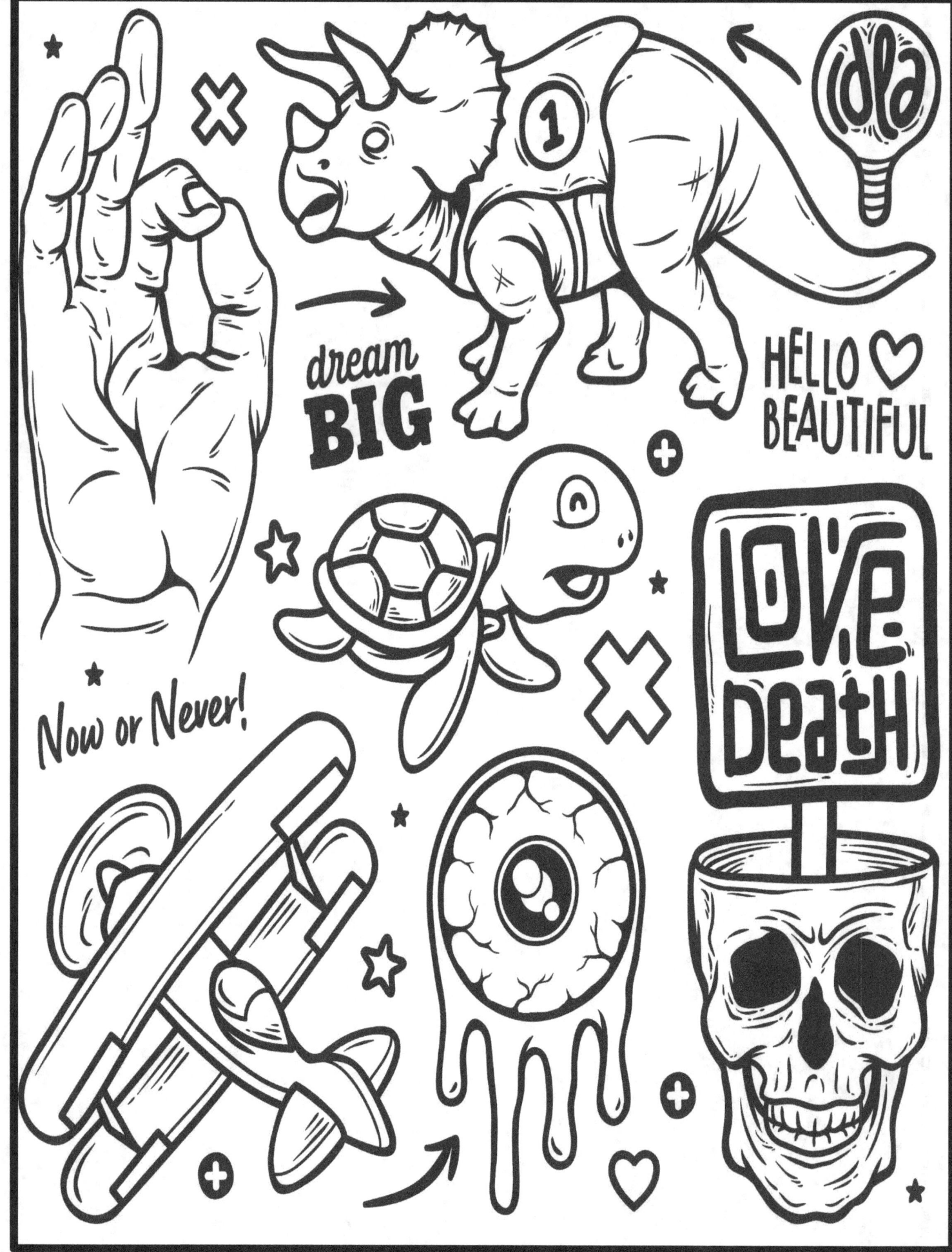

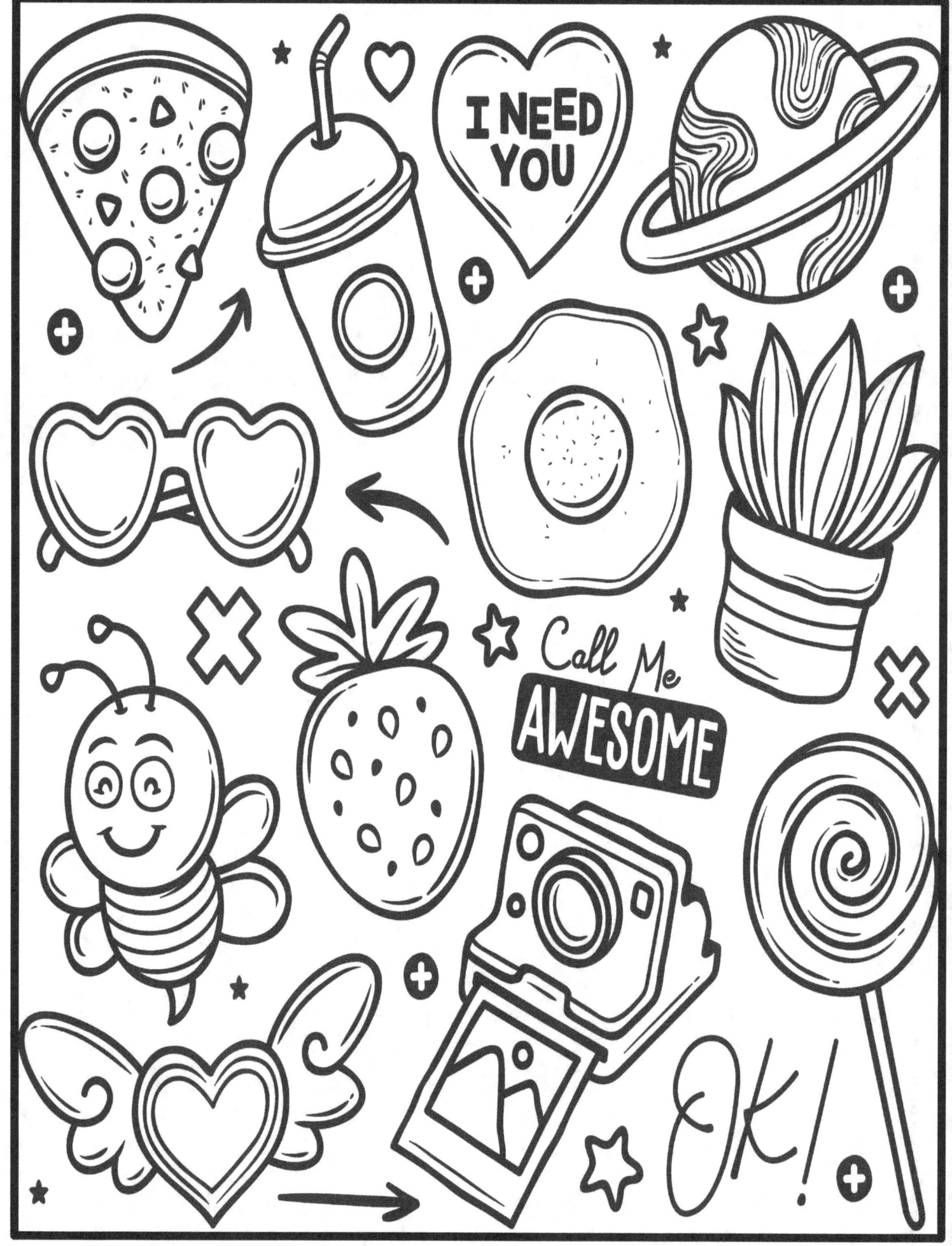

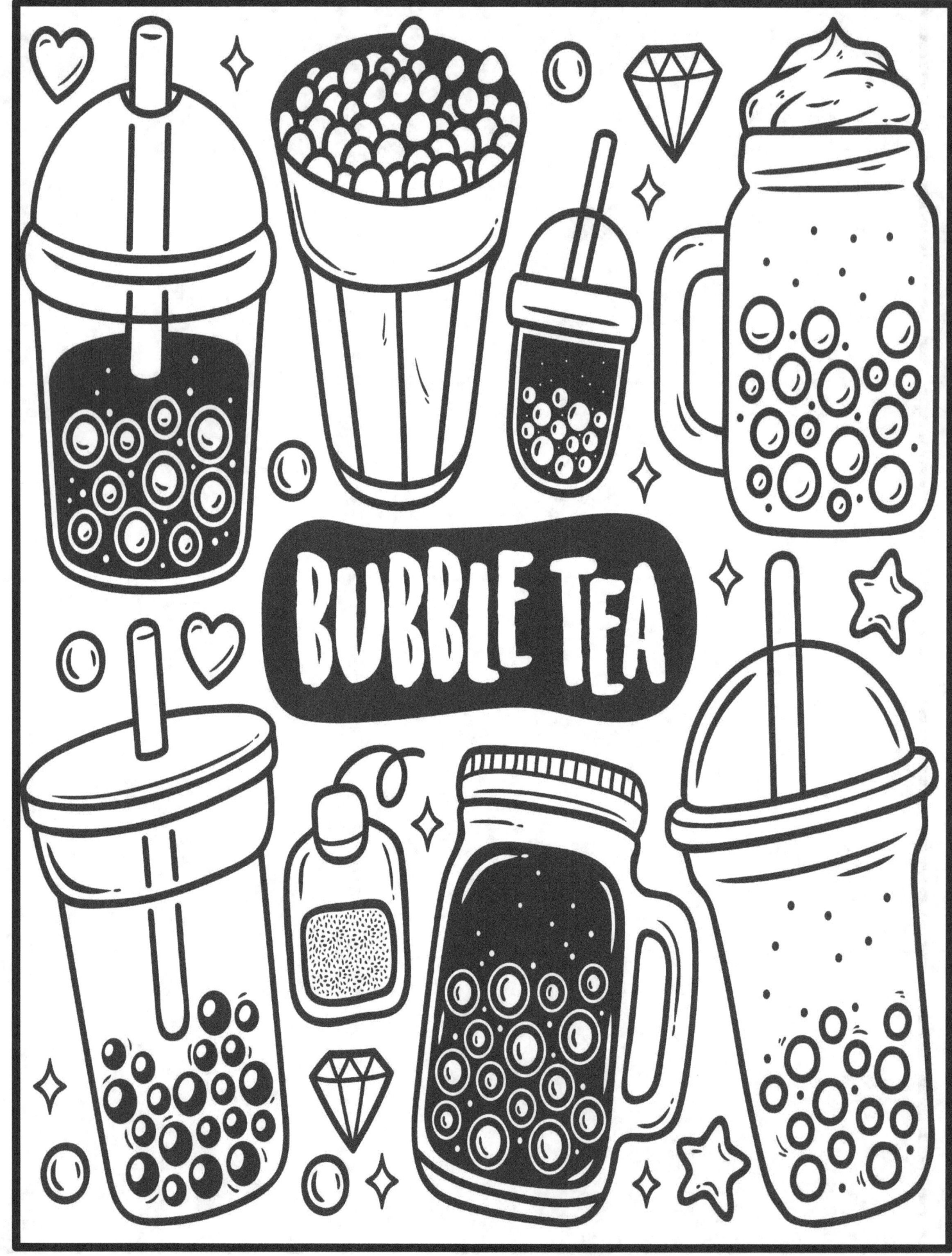

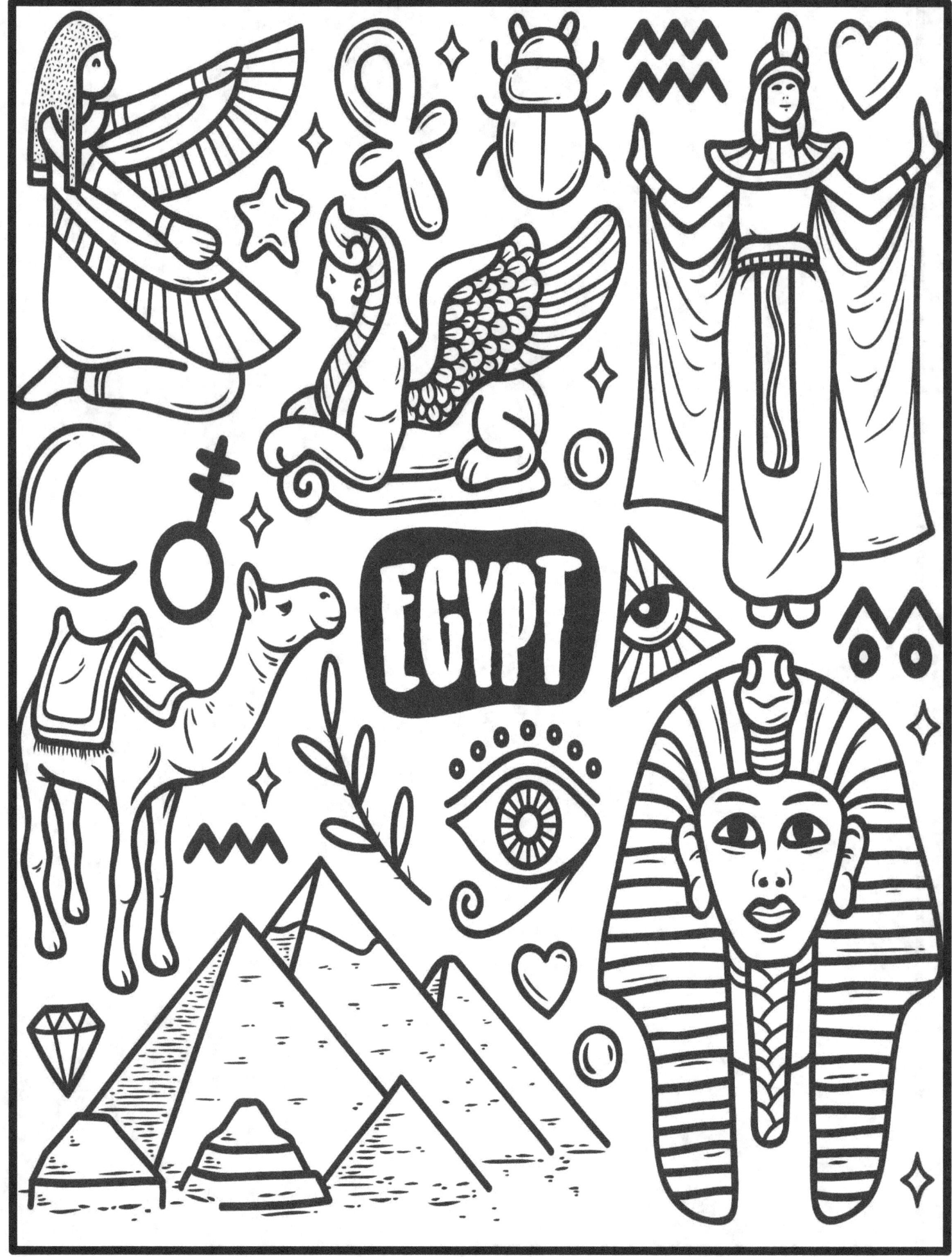

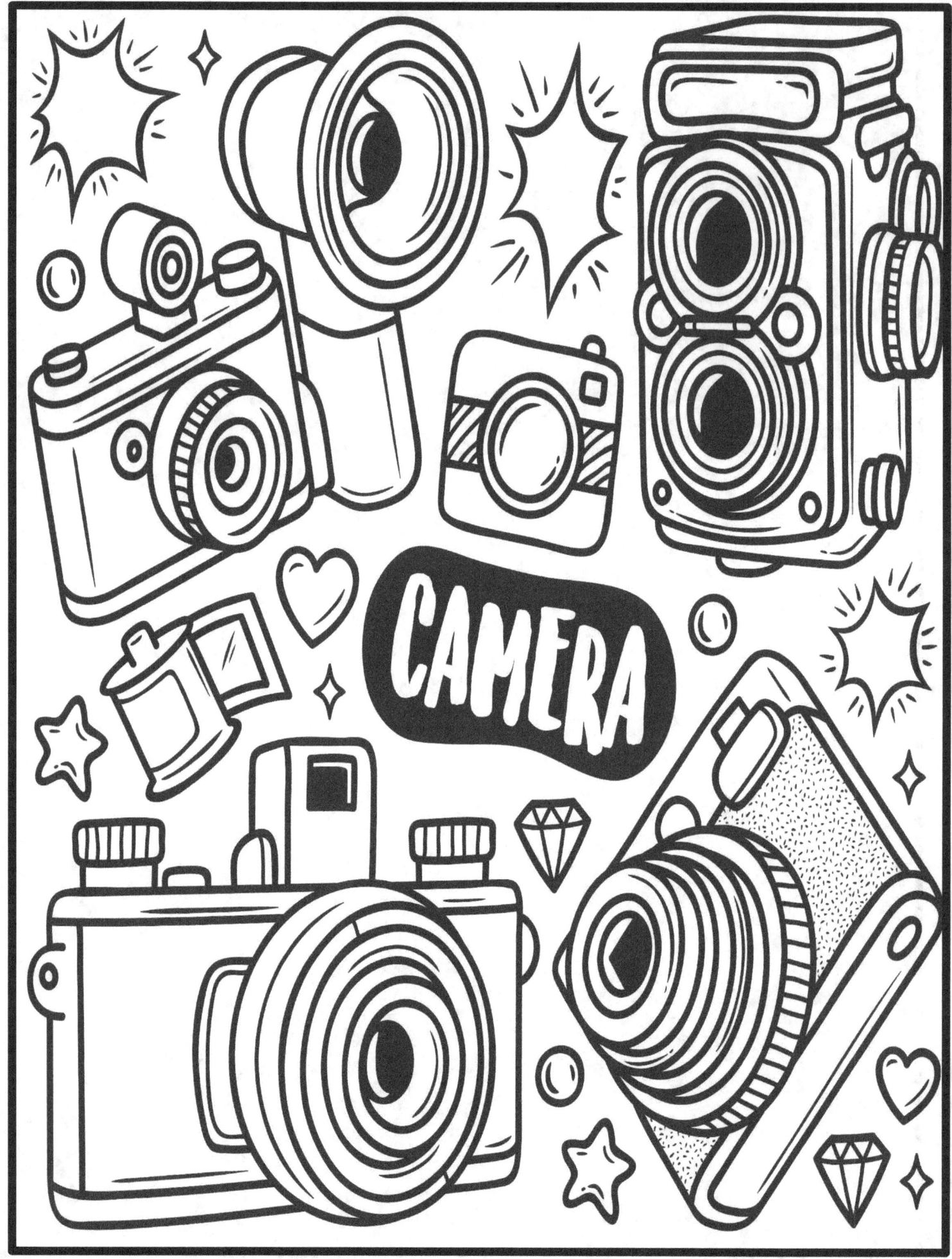

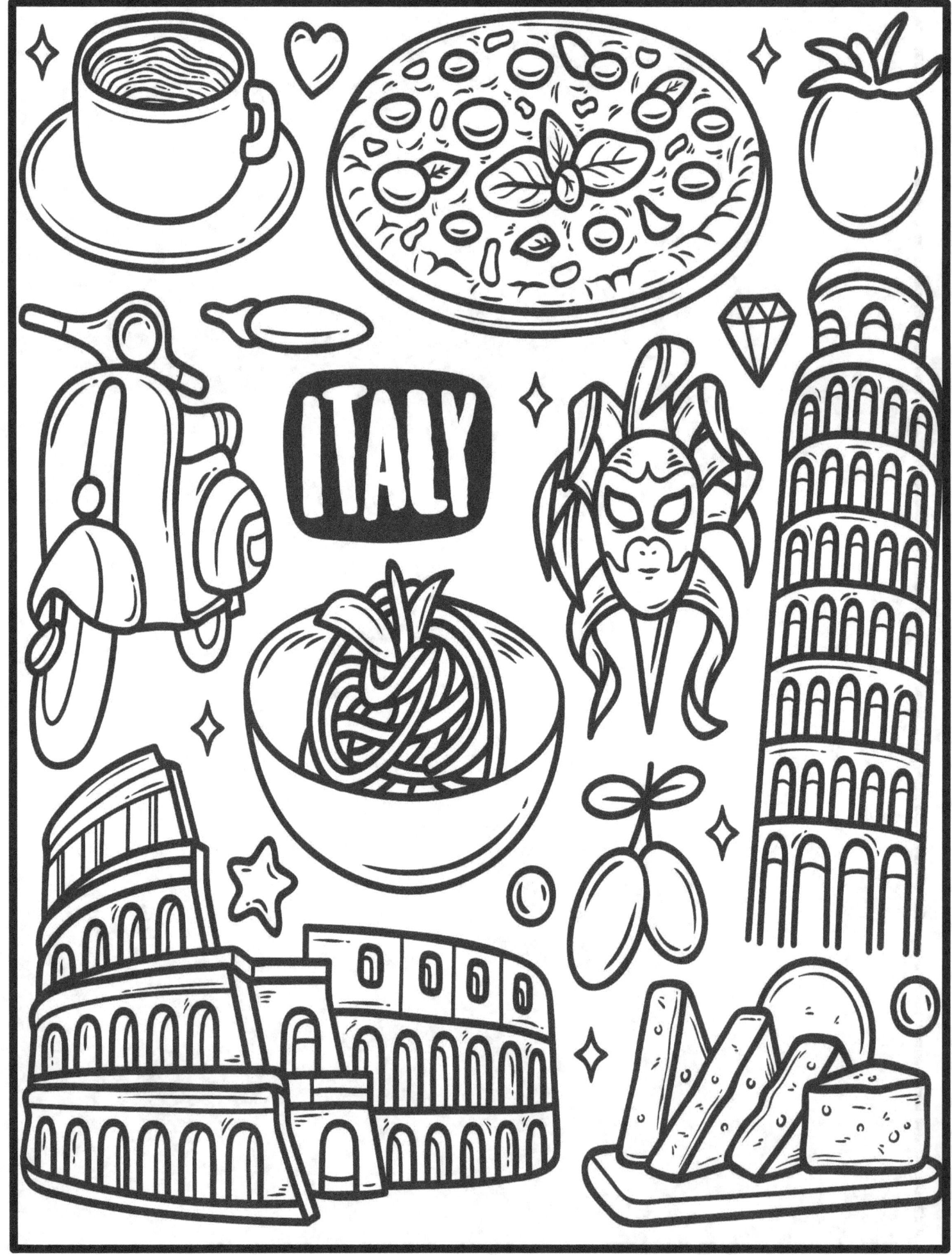

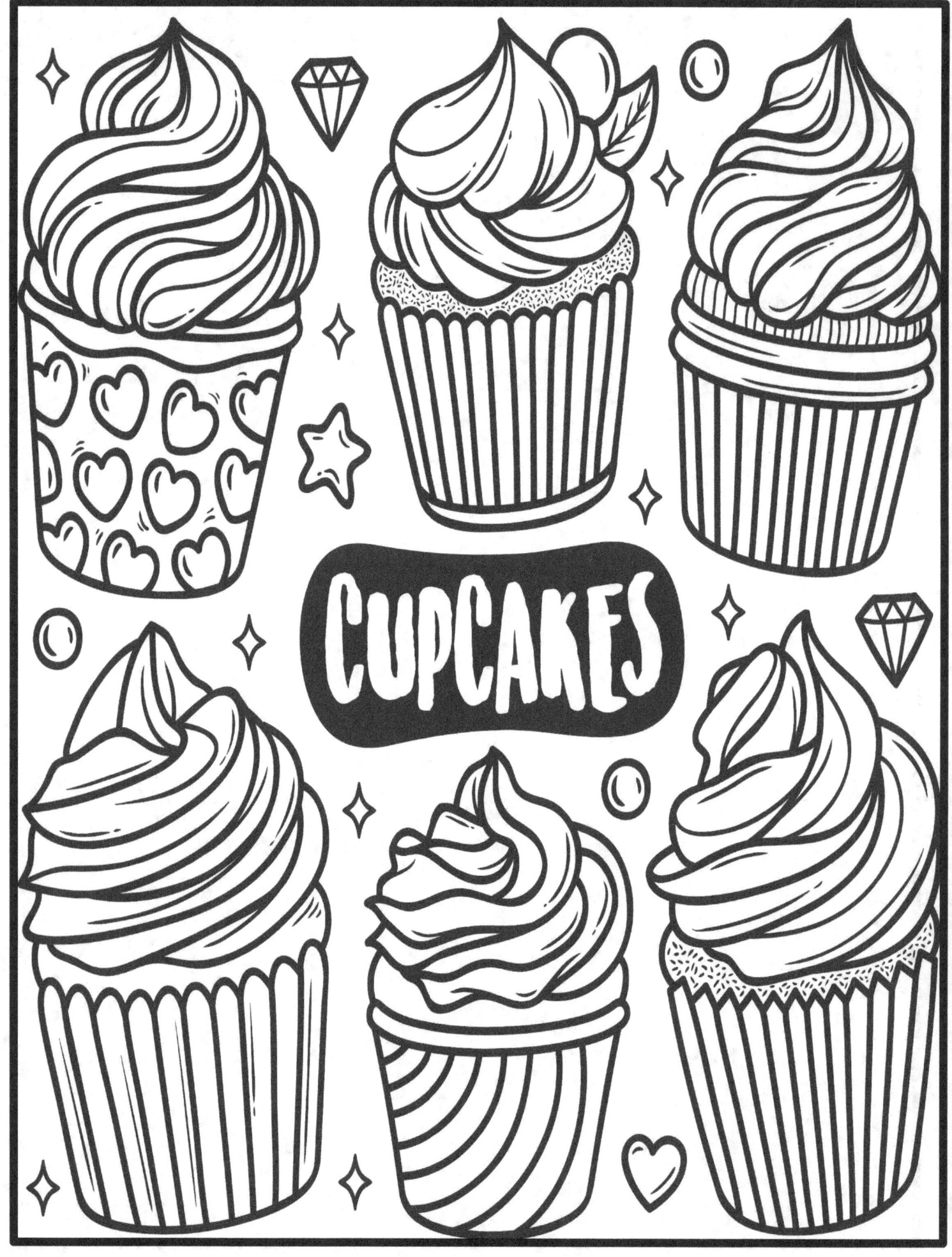

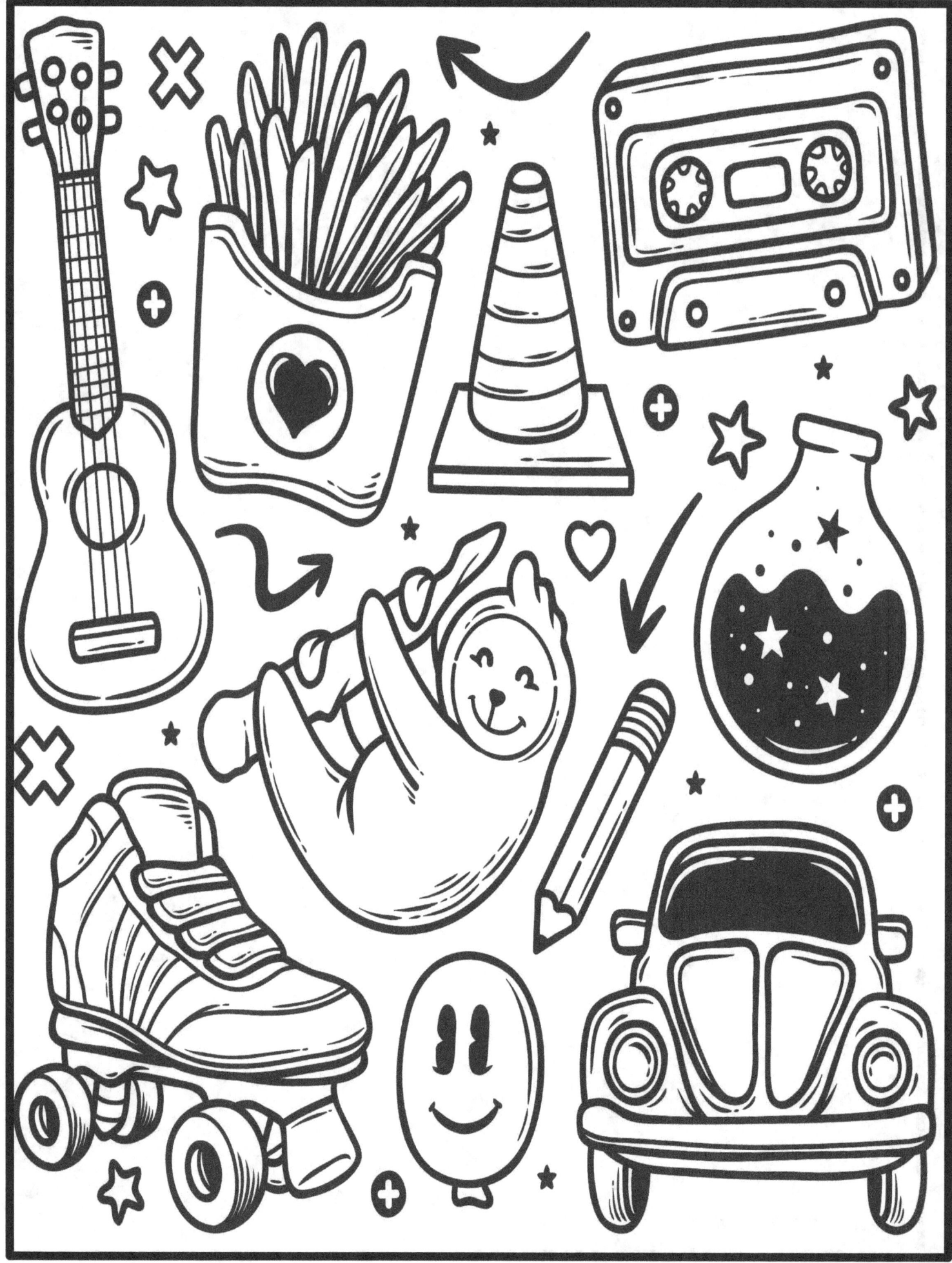

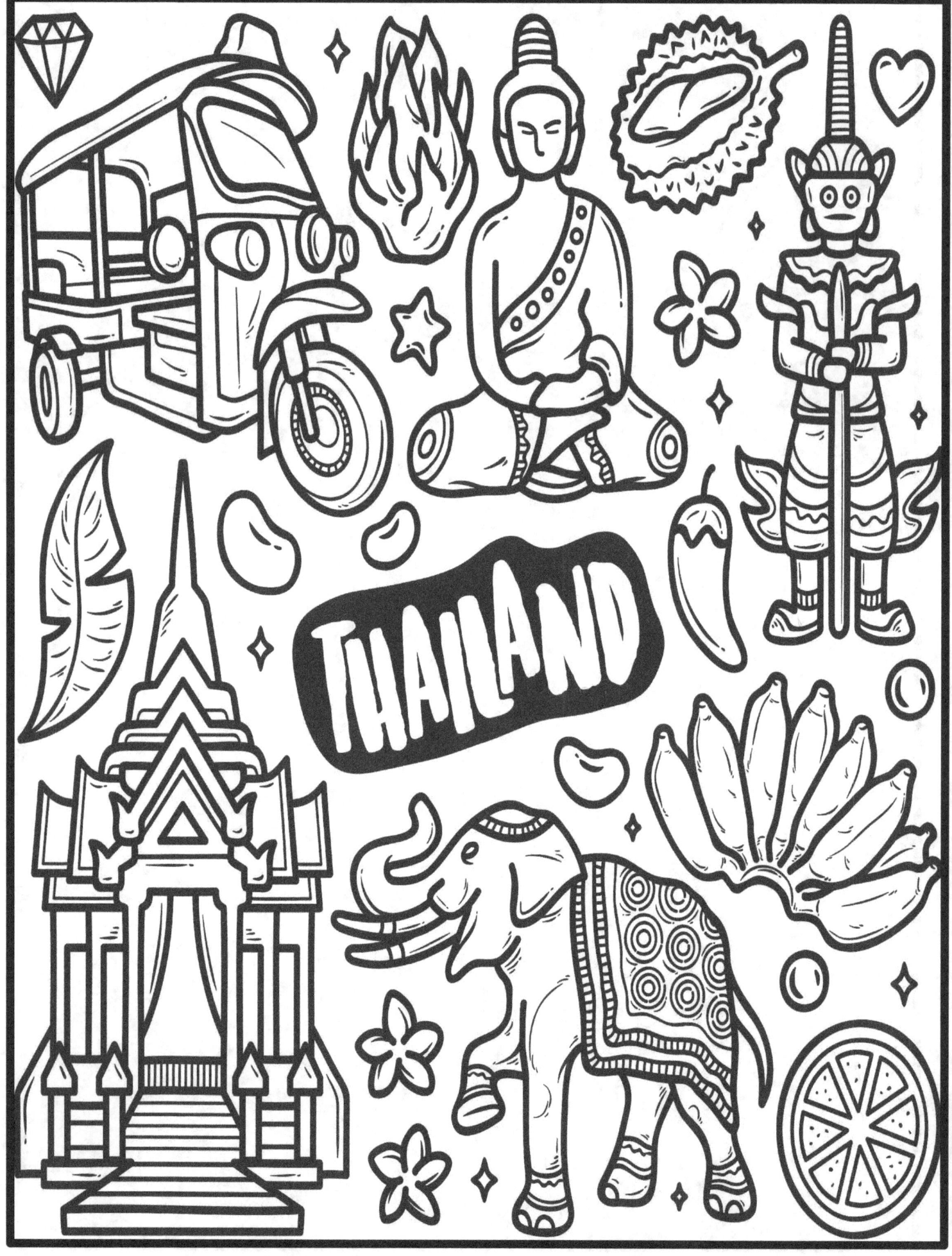

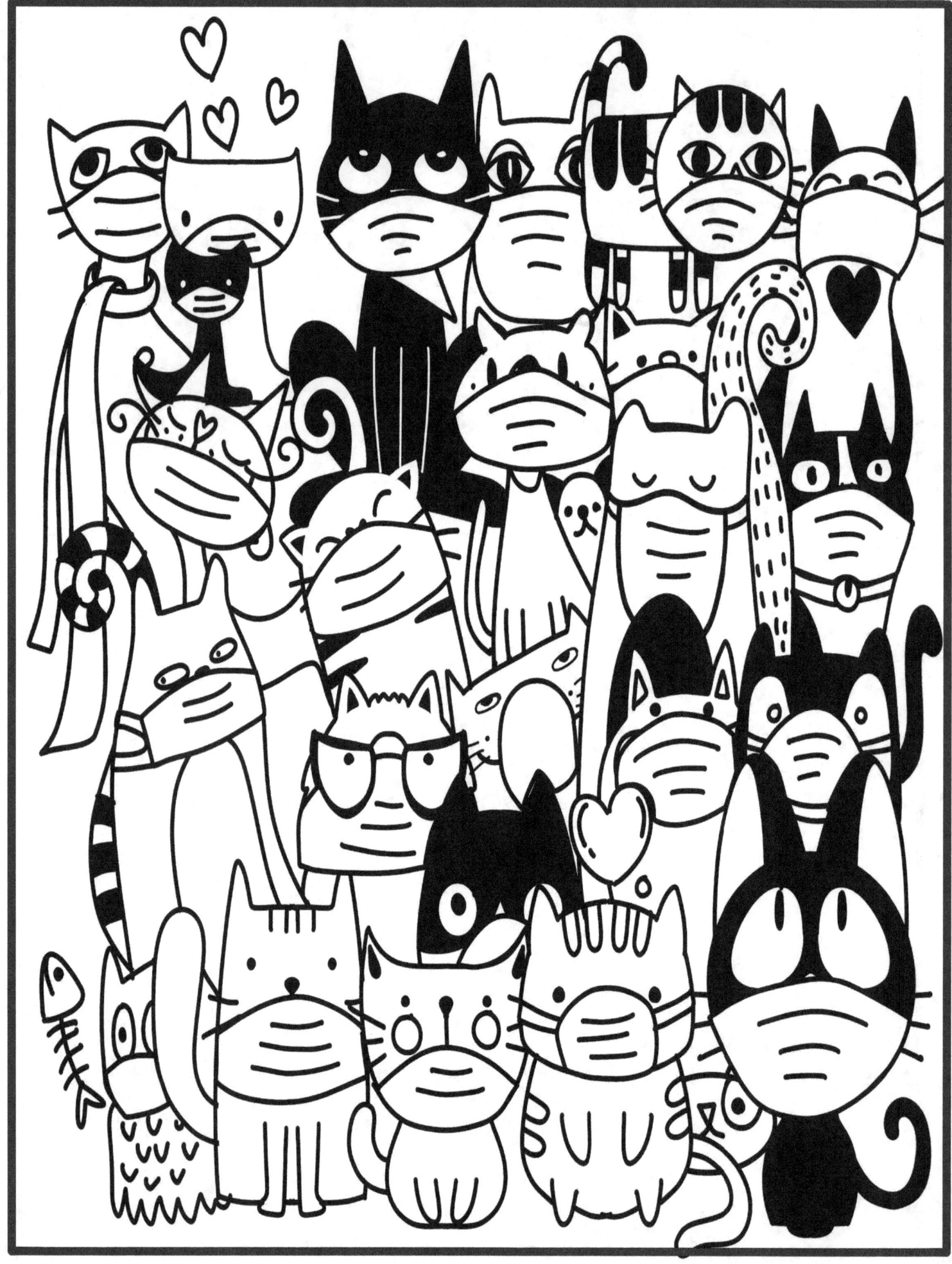

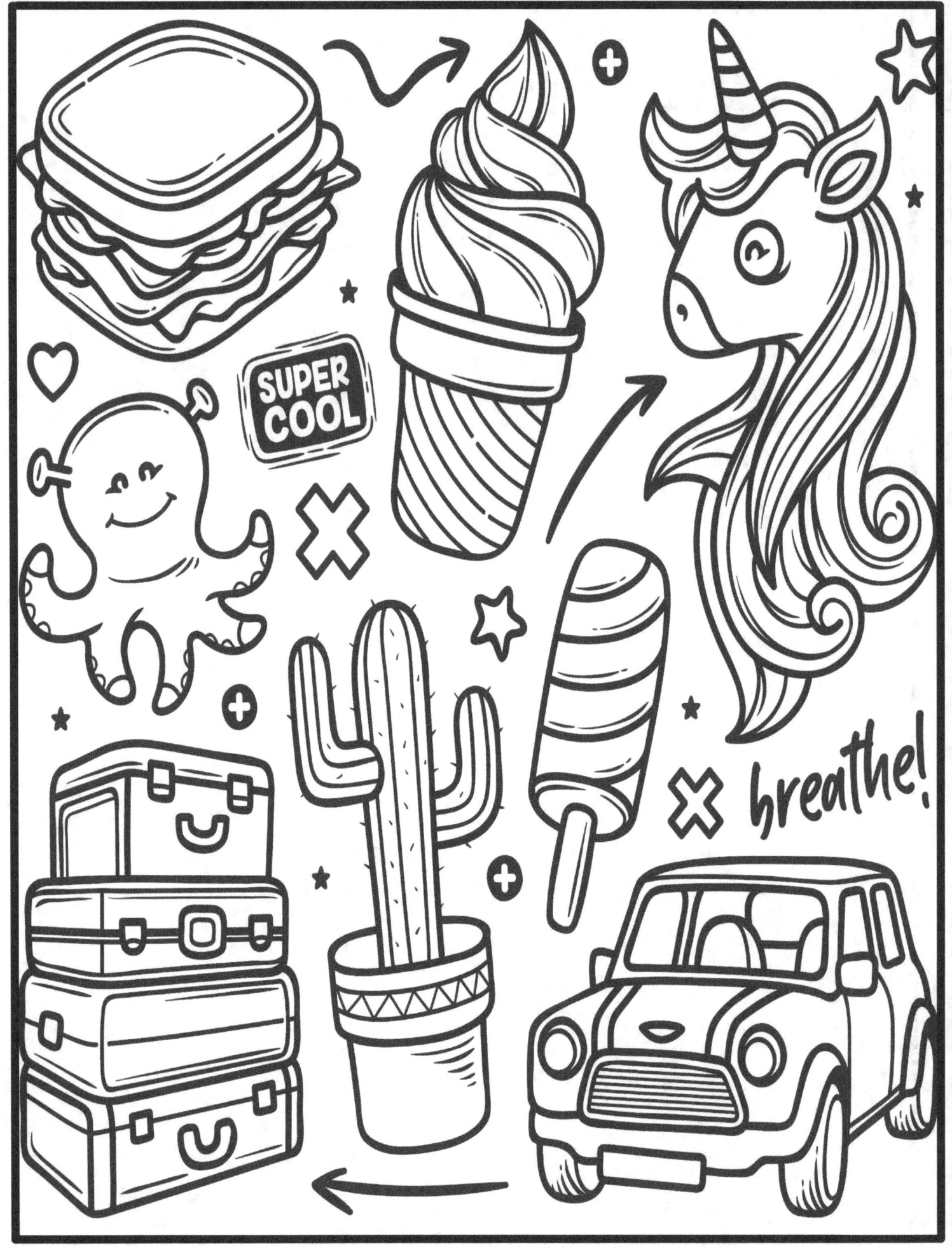

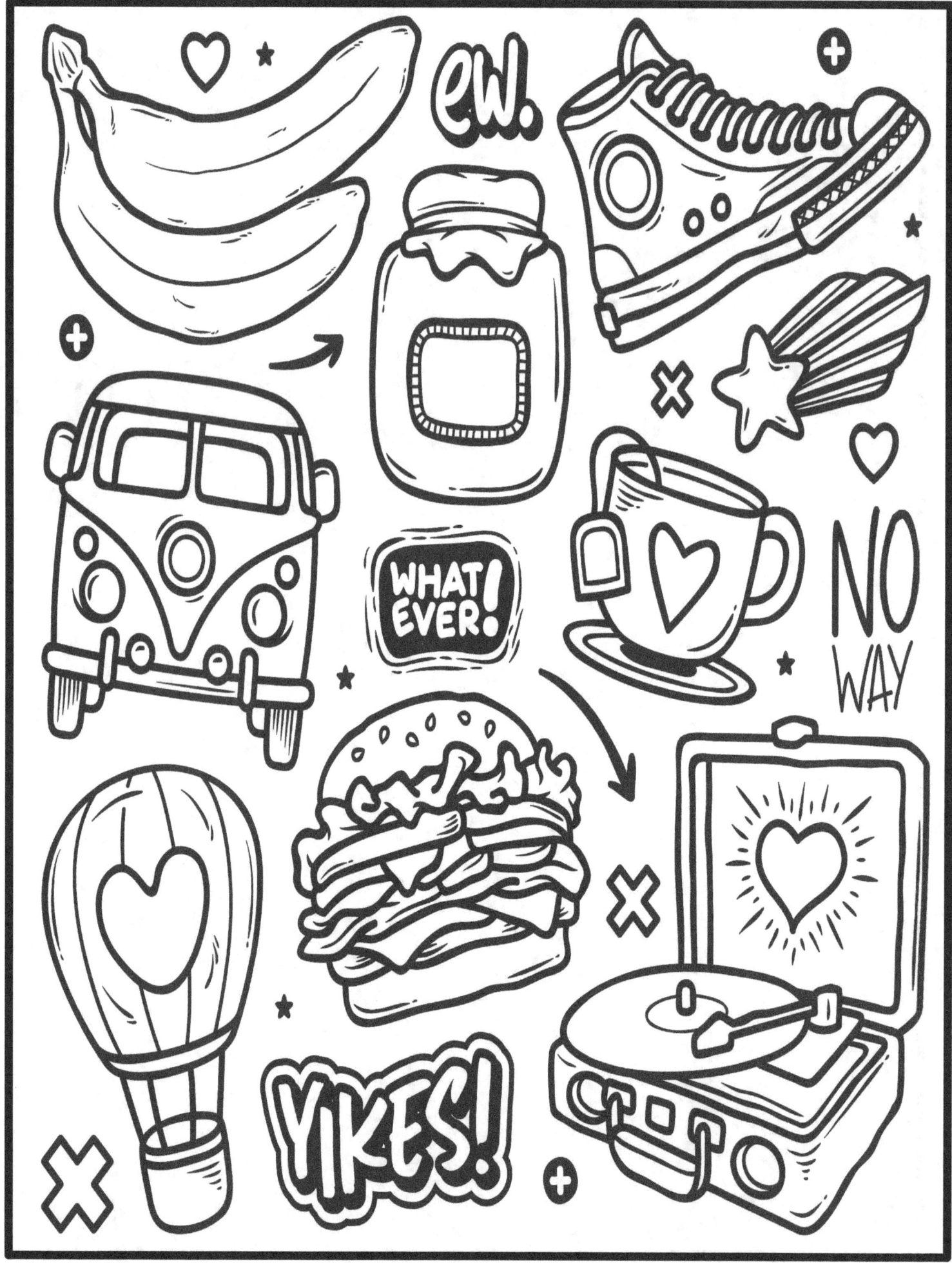

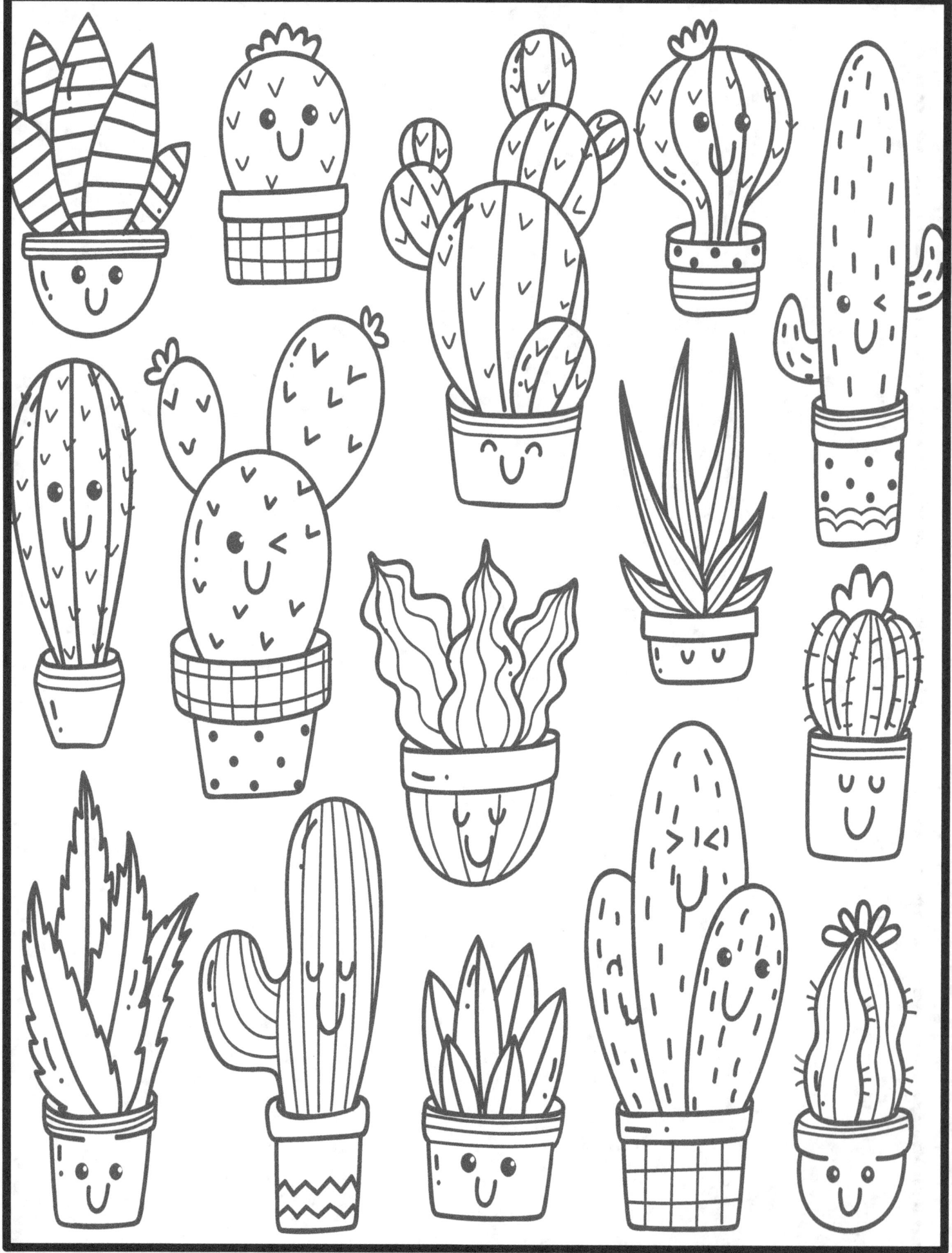

www.ingramcontent.com/pod-product-compliance
Lightning Source LLC
Chambersburg PA
CBHW080939220526
45465CB00008BA/3098